Rea~~
& Criti~~

UNL⌀CK

**STUDENT'S BOOK
WITH DIGITAL PACK**

THIRD EDITION

Natasha De Souza, Alan S. Kennedy,
Chris Sowton, with Jessica Williams

CAMBRIDGE

CAMBRIDGE
UNIVERSITY PRESS & ASSESSMENT

Shaftesbury Road, Cambridge CB2 8EA, United Kingdom

One Liberty Plaza, 20th Floor, New York, NY 10006, USA

477 Williamstown Road, Port Melbourne, VIC 3207, Australia

314–321, 3rd Floor, Plot 3, Splendor Forum, Jasola District Centre, New Delhi – 110025, India

103 Penang Road, #05-06/07, Visioncrest Commercial, Singapore 238467

Cambridge University Press & Assessment is a department of the University of Cambridge.

We share the University's mission to contribute to society through the pursuit of education, learning and research at the highest international levels of excellence.

www.cambridge.org
Information on this title: www.cambridge.org/9781009797566

© Cambridge University Press & Assessment 2025

First published 2014
Second Edition 2019
Second Edition update published 2021
Third Edition 2025

20 19 18 17 16 15 14 13 12 11 10 9 8 7 6 5 4 3 2 1

Printed in Dubai by Oriental Press

A catalogue record for this publication is available from the British Library

ISBN 978-1-009-79756-6 Reading, Writing and Critical Thinking Student's Book with Digital Pack 4
ISBN 978-1-009-53615-8 Reading, Writing and Critical Thinking Student's eBook with Digital Pack 4

CONTENTS

MAP OF THE BOOK

UNIT	VIDEO	READING	VOCABULARY	
1 GLOBALIZATION Reading 1: IKEA's global success (Business) Reading 2: Changing eating habits in Italy (Economics / Cultural studies)	China plans revival of Silk Road trade routes	*Key reading skill:* Making predictions from a text type Topic sentences *Additional skills:* Understanding key vocabulary Using your knowledge Reading for main ideas Reading for detail Making inferences Identifying purpose and audience Synthesizing	Academic alternatives to phrasal verbs Globalization vocabulary	
2 EDUCATION Reading 1: University courses: a traditional degree vs a degree apprenticeship (Education / Sociology) Reading 2: Distance learning vs face-to-face learning (Education)	Global literacy campaigns	*Key reading skill:* Making inferences *Additional skills:* Understanding key vocabulary Using your knowledge Reading for main ideas Reading for detail Synthesizing	Education vocabulary Academic vocabulary	
3 MEDICINE Reading 1: The homeopathy debate (Medical ethics) Reading 2: Should healthcare be free? (Economics)	Doctors using VR to help patients	*Key reading skill:* Annotating a text *Additional skills:* Understanding key vocabulary Using your knowledge Skimming Reading for main ideas Reading for detail Identifying opinions Scanning to find key words Making inferences Synthesizing	Medical vocabulary Academic vocabulary	
4 THE ENVIRONMENT Reading 1: Disaster mitigation (Meteorology) Reading 2: Going Green in Denmark (Environment)	Population and water	*Key reading skill:* Identifying cohesive devices *Additional skills:* Understanding key vocabulary Using your knowledge Predicting content using visuals Skimming Reading for main ideas Reading for detail Making inferences Synthesizing	Academic noun phrases Natural disaster vocabulary	

GRAMMAR	CRITICAL THINKING	WRITING
Grammar for writing: Noun phrases Time phrases	Evaluating supporting examples Using tables and diagrams	*Academic writing skills:* Essay structure Writing an effective thesis statement *Writing task type:* Write an explanatory essay. *Writing task:* How has globalization changed your country?
Grammar for writing: Comparison and contrast language: • Transitions to show comparison and contrast • Adverb clauses of contrast	Analyzing similarities and differences Using a Venn diagram	*Academic writing skills:* Avoiding run-on sentences and comma splices Comparison and contrast essays *Writing task type:* Write a comparison and contrast essay. *Writing task:* Discuss the similarities and differences between studying a language and studying Mathematics.
Grammar for writing: Articles Transitions to show concession	Evaluating ideas	*Academic writing skills:* Sentence variety *Writing task type:* Write an opinion essay *Writing task:* Some people believe that disease prevention is the responsibility of the individual, while others believe it is the role of the government. Discuss both views and give your opinion.
Grammar for writing: Expressing solutions using *it*	Analyzing a case study Evaluating arguments	*Academic writing skills:* Developing ideas Parallel structure *Writing task type:* Write a problem-solution essay *Writing task:* Choose a case study of a natural disaster. Write an essay about the problems it caused and provide both short and long-term solutions, taking cost into consideration.

UNIT	VIDEO	READING	VOCABULARY
5 ARCHITECTURE Reading 1: We need more green buildings (Environmental planning) Reading 2: Building design: form vs function (Building design)	Government grants for warmer, cheaper housing	*Key reading skill:* Skimming a text *Additional skills:* Understanding key vocabulary Using your knowledge Reading for detail Understanding paraphrase Making inferences Synthesizing	Academic word families Architecture and planning vocabulary
6 ENERGY Reading 1: Renewable energy (Energy development) Reading 2: The pros and cons of the electric car (Environment / technology)	The power of the wind	*Key reading skill:* Working out meaning from context *Additional skills:* Understanding key vocabulary Using your knowledge Predicting content using visuals Reading for main ideas Reading for detail Making inferences Synthesizing	Energy collocations Formal and informal academic verbs
7 ART AND DESIGN Reading 1: All that art is (Fine art) Reading 2: Photography as art (Photography)	Beijing Art Zone	*Key reading skill:* Scanning to find information *Additional skills:* Understanding key vocabulary Using your knowledge Predicting content using visuals Reading for detail Making inferences Understanding paraphrase Synthesizing	Vocabulary for art and design
8 AGEING Reading 1: The social and economic impact of ageing (Economics) Reading 2: What are the impacts of a young population on a society? (Social anthropology)	The happiest time of your life?	*Key reading skill:* Identifying evidence in a text *Additional skills:* Understanding key vocabulary Using your knowledge Reading for main ideas Reading for detail Working out meaning Synthesizing	Academic collocations with prepositions

GRAMMAR	CRITICAL THINKING	WRITING
Grammar for writing: Register in academic writing	Creating a persuasive argument	*Academic writing skills:* Ordering information Writing a persuasive argument *Writing task type:* Write a persuasive essay *Writing task:* Which is more important when building or buying a new home: its location or its size?
Grammar for writing: Relative clauses	Evaluating benefits and drawbacks Organizing ideas for an essay	*Academic writing skills:* Introducing advantages and disadvantages Coherence *Writing task type:* Write an advantages and disadvantages essay *Writing task:* Explain the advantages and disadvantages of three types of renewable energy and decide which would work best in your country.
Paraphrasing quotations *Grammar for writing:* Substitution Ellipsis	Understanding and evaluating analogies	*Academic writing skills:* Arguments, counter-arguments and refutations *Writing task type:* Write an argumentative essay *Writing task:* Fashion, cooking and video games have all been likened to fine art. Choose *one* of these and discuss whether it should be considered fine art, comparable to painting or sculpture.
Cause and effect *Grammar for writing:* Language of prediction The first conditional	Drawing appropriate conclusions from graphical data	*Academic writing skills:* Numerical words and phrases Interpreting graphs and charts *Writing task type:* Write an analysis essay *Writing task:* Describe population trends in Japan. Use the data from the graph as evidence to support your claims. Suggest the potential impact on the country if the 2050 projections are correct.

UNLOCK YOUR ACADEMIC POTENTIAL

Unlock Third Edition is a six-level, academic-light English course created to build the skills and language students need for their studies (CEFR Pre-A1 to C1). It develops students' ability to think critically in an academic context right from the start of their language learning. Every level has inspiring videos on a range of academic topics.

CRITICAL THINKING

Unlock Third Edition includes the right mix of lower- and higher-order thinking skills development in every unit, with clear learning objectives. Students are better prepared for their academic studies and have the confidence to apply the critical thinking skills they have developed. Critical thinking in *Unlock Third Edition*:

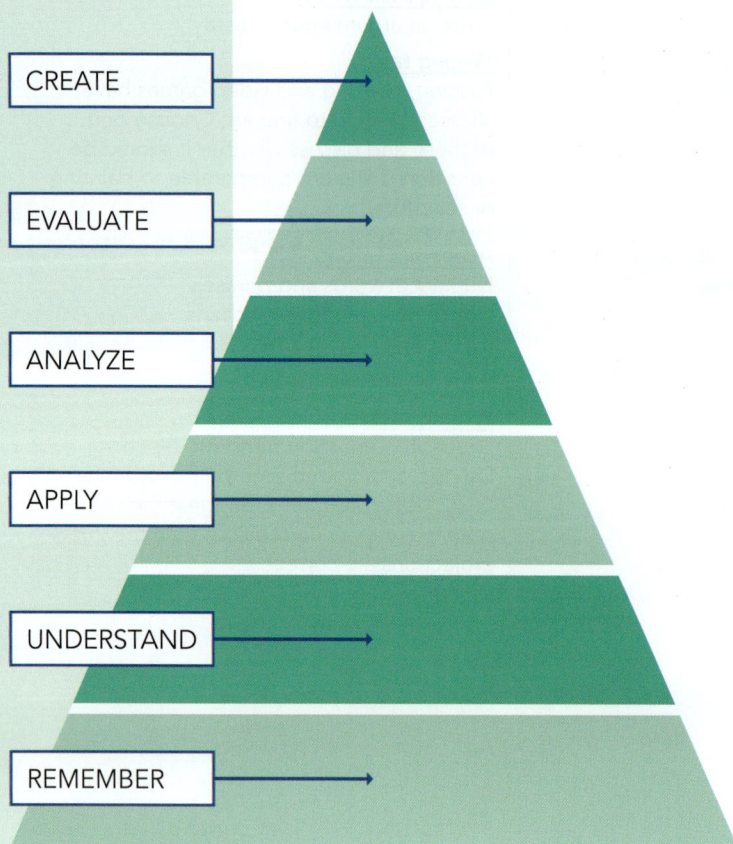

CREATE

EVALUATE

ANALYZE

APPLY

UNDERSTAND

REMEMBER

- is **informed** by a range of academic research from Bloom in the 1950s, to Krathwohl and Anderson in the 2000s, to more recent considerations relating to 21st Century Skills

- has a **refined** syllabus with a better mix of higher- and lower-order critical thinking skills

- is **measurable**, with objectives and self-evaluation so students can track their critical thinking progress

- is **transparent** so teachers and students know when and why they're developing critical thinking skills

- is **supported** with professional development material for teachers so teachers can teach with confidence

TEACHER RESOURCES

We've carried out research with teachers across the world to understand their needs and how we can better meet them with *Unlock*. All teacher resources can be accessed on our learning platform, Cambridge One cambridge.org/one.

- Fully interactive presentation software, **Presentation Plus**, with pop-up activities to type or automatically display answers.
- Downloadable **Model Answer Booklet** with model answers for all end-of-unit productive activities and example answers for all 'Answers may vary' activity types in the Student's Book.
- **Variations of unit tests, mid- and end-of-course tests** give teachers options when assessing student understanding and progress.
- **Teacher Manual and Development Pack** supports your teaching with flexible lesson plans with timings for every unit.
- **Digital Workbook with videos** to assign additional practice for your students whenever you see this symbol

RESEARCH

Unlock Third Edition is informed by consulting with a global advisory panel and comprehensive review of the material so you can be assured of the quality of every lesson.

- **extensive market research** with teachers and students to fully understand their needs throughout the course's development
- consulting **academic research** into critical thinking
- refined vocabulary syllabus using our **exclusive Corpus research** ☉

UNL🔗CK YOUR KNOWLEDGE

Work with a partner. Discuss the questions.

1 Look at the photo. What do you think the people are studying?
2 What do you think of the education system in your country? What do you think works well and what could be improved?
3 How do you think your education system could become more modernized and useful for today's generation? Think about new subjects, and technology for the classroom.
4 At what age can students leave school in your country? What type of exams do you have to take before you leave school?

WATCH AND LISTEN

ACTIVATING YOUR KNOWLEDGE

PREPARING TO WATCH
1 Work with a partner and answer the questions.
1 How do you think your life would be different if you were unable

Unlock your knowledge
Encourages discussion around the themes of the unit with inspiration from interesting questions and striking images.

Watch and listen
Features an engaging and motivating video which generates interest in the topic and develops listening skills.

READING

READING 1

PREDICTING CONTENT USING

PREPARING TO READ
1 You are going to read an essay with the title *A Traditional Degree Versus a Degree Apprenticeship*. Look at the photos. Which

READING 2

UNDERSTANDING KEY VOCABULARY

PREPARING TO READ
1 You are going to read an article about distance and face-to-face learning. Before you read, match the collocations to their meanings.

1 core principles	a recent trend
2 credible alternative	b important distinction
3 distance learning	c an academic qualification obtained from online instruction
4 modern phenomenon	d key values
5 online degree	e general education from online instruction
6 significant difference	f online course
7 technological advances	g reliable substitute
8 virtual classroom	h developments in technology

2 Complete the sentences and discuss your answers with a partner.
1 One interesting **modern phenomenon** in my country is _____.

Reading 1
Offers students the opportunity to develop the reading skills required to process academic texts, and presents and practises the vocabulary needed to comprehend the text itself.

Reading 2
Provides a different angle on the topic and serves as a model text for the writing task.

⊙ LANGUAGE DEVELOPMENT

EDUCATION VOCABULARY

> assignment campus degree dissertation examination
> journal lecturer plagiarism seminar term tutor

1 Complete the statements with some of the words from the box. Then circle the option in *italics* to give your own opinion.
1 If a student commits _____ by copying from their sources, or by not acknowledging them, when writing an essay, they *should / should not* be removed from the course immediately.
2 Research papers, known as _____ *should / should not* be available free of charge to students from poorer backgrounds.
3 When you need to pass a formal _____ to get a specific qualification, you should revise *on your own / with peers*.
4 When I am given an _____ to complete, I usually *manage / do not manage* to hand it in on time.

UNIVERSITY COURSES:
A TRADITIONAL DEGREE VS A DEGREE APPRENTICESHIP

1 Traditional university degrees have been valued for hundreds of years. A university education allows graduates to make better choices by increasing job opportunities for a broad range of careers. Research shows that men with a university education can earn salaries of around 8% more than their **peers** and for graduate women the gap is even bigger at 28%. It is not surprising, therefore, that university is the most popular higher education option with nearly eight hundred thousand school-leavers starting a degree course in 2023. However, even though a traditional degree is extremely beneficial, it can still be extremely challenging for graduates to find a job due to a lack of work experience. Degree apprenticeships, which were introduced in the UK in 2015, are realistic alternatives to gaining a degree qualification, particularly with school-leavers who

3 Research suggests that one of the main advantages graduate apprentices have over their peers is that they learn key workplace skills. During their apprenticeship students will attend meetings and meet **deadlines**. They will build valuable relationships with colleagues at many different levels and may even communicate with external [2]stakeholders like customers. These [3]'soft skills', for example,

Language development
Consolidates and expands on the language presented in preparation for the writing task.

QR codes
Allow students to easily access the audio of the reading passages.

WRITING

CRITICAL THINKING

At the end of this unit, you are going to write a comparison and contrast essay. Look at this unit's writing task below.

Discuss the various similarities and differences between studying a language and studying Mathematics.

1 Look at the two ideas maps below. One is labelled 'Studying a language' and the other 'Studying Mathematics'. Add details according to your experience of studying these subjects.

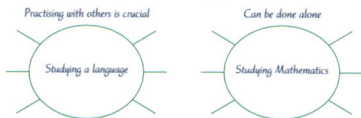

UNDERSTAND

Practising with others is crucial

Studying a language

Can be done alone

Studying Mathematics

Critical thinking
Develops the lower- and higher-order thinking skills required for the writing task.

GRAMMAR FOR WRITING

COMPARISON AND CONTRAST LANGUAGE

GRAMMAR

Transitions to show comparison and contrast
The ability to **compare** similar ideas or to **contrast** different ideas is an important skill in academic writing.
Students in face-to-face courses see tutors often. Similarly, *students in distance-learning courses contact their tutors in online forums often.*
Universities charge high fees for academic subjects. However, *colleges charge much less for vocational courses.*
Words such as *however* and *similarly* are called **transition words**. When transition words begin a sentence, they must be followed by a **comma**.

1 Complete the table with transition words or phrases from the box.

| although   compared to   conversely   equally |
| however   in contrast   in the same way   nevertheless |
| on the other hand   similarly |

Grammar for writing
Presents and practises grammatical structures and features needed for the writing task.

ACADEMIC WRITING SKILLS

AVOIDING RUN-ON SENTENCES AND COMMA SPLICES

Run-on sentences and comma splices are common errors that writers must know how to avoid in academic writing. If they are used incorrectly, they can make it difficult for the reader to understand what you mean.

What is a run-on sentence?
A run on sentence is two independent clauses that have not been connected in the right way.

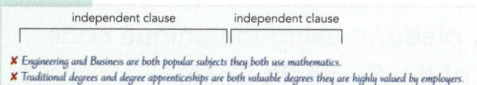

| independent clause | independent clause |

✗ *Engineering and Business are both popular subjects they both use mathematics.*
✗ *Traditional degrees and degree apprenticeships are both valuable degrees they are highly valued by employers.*

This sentence is incorrect because it is missing a word to link the

Academic writing skills
Practises all the writing skills needed for the writing task.

WRITING TASK

Discuss the various similarities and differences between studying a language and studying Mathematics. Write about 350–400 words.

PLAN
1 Look back at the Venn diagram in Critical thinking with your notes on the similarities and differences between studying a language and studying Mathematics. Now take those ideas, plus any new ones you can think of, and create an outline for your essay using the structure below.

	Your notes
Introductory paragraph: (background information, thesis statement) (about 50–100 words)	*Maths and languages are two important subjects which many people choose to study at university. While Maths is ….*
Body paragraph 1: (differences)	*When comparing the two subjects, the most obvious*

Writing task
Uses the skills and language learned throughout the unit to support students in drafting, producing and editing a piece of academic writing. This is the unit's main learning objective.

OBJECTIVES REVIEW

1 Check your learning objectives for this unit. Write *3*, *2* or *1* for each objective.

3 = very well   2 = well   1 = not so well

I can …

watch and understand a video about global literacy campaigns. ____

make inferences and analyze similarities and differences. ____

use a Venn diagram to plan a comparison-contrast essay. ____

use transitions to show comparison and contrast. ____

use adverb clauses of contrast. ____

avoid run-on sentences and comma splices. ____

write a comparison and contrast essay. ____

Objectives review
Allows students to evaluate how well they have mastered the skills covered in the unit.

WORDLIST

alternative (n) ⊙	distance learning (n phr)	principle (adj)
aspect (n) ⊙		pursue (v) ⊙
assignment (n) ⊙	employability (n)	regard (v) ⊙
campus (n) ⊙	establishment (n) ⊙	semester (n)
community (n) ⊙	examination (n) ⊙	seminar (n) ⊙
concrete (adj)	in-depth (adj)	significant (adj)
core (adj)	illiteracy (n)	specific (adj)
core principles (n phr)	journal (n) ⊙	stigma (n) ⊙
credible alternative (n phr)	lecturer (n) ⊙	technological advances (n phr)
deadline (n)	modern phenomenon (n phr)	term (n) ⊙
degree (n) ⊙	motivation (n) ⊙	tutor (n) ⊙
discipline (n) ⊙	online degree (n phr)	virtual (adj)
dissertation (n) ⊙	peer (n) ⊙	virtual classroom (n phr)
	plagiarism (n)	

⊙ = high-frequency words in the Cambridge Academic Corpus

Wordlist
Lists the key vocabulary from the unit. The most frequent words used at this level in an academic context are highlighted with this icon ⊙

Unlock offers 70–90 hours per Student's Book, which is extendable with the Digital Pack, and other additional activities in the Teacher's Manual and Development Pack.

Unlock is a paired-skills course with two separate Student's Books per level. For levels 1–5 (CEFR A1–C1), these are **Reading, Writing and Critical Thinking** and **Listening, Speaking and Critical Thinking**. They share the same unit topics so you have access to a wide range of material at each level. Each Student's Book includes access to the Digital Pack.

Unlock Basic has been developed for pre-A1 learners. **Unlock Basic Skills** integrates reading, writing, listening, speaking and critical thinking in one book to provide students with an effective and manageable learning experience. **Unlock Basic Literacy** develops and builds confidence in literacy. The Basic books also share the same unit topics and so can be used together or separately, and **Unlock Basic Literacy** can be used for self-study.

STUDENT COMPONENTS

All material in the Student's Digital Pack (Levels 1–5) can be accessed on Cambridge One, our learning platform using the unique code printed on the inside front cover of the Student's Book.

Resource	Description

Student's Book with Digital Pack	• 8 units per level (Levels 1–4); 10 units (Level 5)
	• QR codes for students to easily access the Class Audio
	• Levels 1–5 includes access to the Digital Pack:
	  – Interactive eBook with videos
	  – Digital Workbook
	  – Downloadable audio for listening activities and pronunciation (Listening and Speaking strand)
	  – Downloadable audio for reading passages (Reading and Writing strand)
	• *Unlock Basic Skills* comes with downloadable audio and video (11 units)
	• *Unlock Basic Literacy* comes with downloadable audio (11 units)

Interactive eBook with videos	• Levels 1–5 • Digital version of the Student's Book with auto-graded activities • Student's Book videos for students to watch on their own
Digital Workbook with videos	• Levels 1–5 • Extension activities to further practise the language and skills learned • Additional video comprehension and extension activities that are different from the activities in the Student's Book.

TEACHER COMPONENTS

All teacher components can be accessed on Cambridge One, our learning platform. Teachers can access the Digital Workbook with videos by creating an account. To access the Teacher's Resources and Presentation Plus, please request an access code from your local Cambridge representative.

Resource	Description
Audio	• Downloadable audio for listening activities and pronunciation (Listening and Speaking strand) • Downloadable audio for reading passages (Reading and Writing strand)
Teacher's Manual and Development Pack	• Flexible lesson plans with timings, lesson objectives and lesson observation templates • Downloadable Model Answer Booklet with model and example answers for productive skills • Supplementary classroom materials for Levels 1–4 • Common student errors • *Developing critical thinking skills in your students*, a teacher development material with clear objectives, in-practice activities and opportunities for review and self-evaluation.
Teacher Development Resources	Additional materials which can be used for professional development: • Peer-to-peer training workshop materials with PowerPoint presentations • In-session worksheets, trainer's notes • Pre- and post- workshop quizzes
Presentation Plus	• Fully interactive presentation software, with pop-up activities to type or automatically display answers • Embedded audio and video for easy access to play in class
Tests	• Unit, mid- and end-of-course tests for the assessment of student understanding and progress

TEACHING WITH *UNLOCK THIRD EDITION*

This online training course gives you a thorough knowledge of how *Unlock* works, what it includes and acquaints teachers with the methodological principles behind the course.

GLOBALIZATION

LEARNING OBJECTIVES

Watch and listen

Watch and understand a video about China's plans to revive the Silk Road trade routes.

Reading skills

Make predictions from a text type; recognize topic sentences.

Critical thinking

Evaluate supporting examples; use tables and diagrams.

Grammar

Use noun phrases; use time phrases.

Academic writing skill

Use correct essay structure; write an effective thesis statement.

Writing task

Write an explanatory essay.

UNL🔗CK YOUR KNOWLEDGE

Work with a partner. Discuss the questions.

1 What do you think the term *globalization* means?

2 How do you think the products in the images above contribute to globalization?

3 Can you think of any global brands which you use regularly? Do you think these global brands have had a positive or negative effect on your life and society in general?

WATCH AND LISTEN

PREPARING TO WATCH

1 You are going to watch a video about an important transport route. Before you watch, work with a partner and discuss the questions.

1 Where do most of the imported products in your country come from?

2 What products does your country export to other countries?

3 How are these products usually transported in and out of the country? Why?

2 Work with a partner. Look at the pictures from the video and discuss the questions.

1 What kind of location is shown in the first picture? Where do you think it is?

2 What forms of transport do you see in the other pictures? What does it tell you about the location?

3 What do you think they are transporting? Where do you think they are coming from and going to?

GLOSSARY

the Silk Road (n) an ancient trade route mainly across land from China, across central Asia to the Eastern Mediterranean and Europe

dry port (n) a transport centre where goods are loaded and unloaded, but which is not near water

logistics hub (n) a centre where goods are received, stored, and then sent out to different places

infrastructure (n) the basic systems and services, such as transport and power, that a country uses to work effectively

think tank (n) a group of experts who work together to study a problem and suggest solutions

domestic (adj) related to issues inside a country

WHILE WATCHING

3 ▶ Watch the video. Which sentence summarizes the main idea?

UNDERSTANDING MAIN IDEAS

1 The Silk Road is an important part of China's history.
2 The Chinese government is aiming to create a giant trade network to connect Asia and Europe.
3 Korgas could be like other Chinese cities, such as Shanghai.

4 ▶ Watch again. Write *T* (true) or *F* (false) next to the statements below. Correct the false statements.

UNDERSTANDING DETAIL

_____ 1 Korgas in China is the starting point of a new trading route.
_____ 2 Five years ago there wasn't much infrastructure in the area.
_____ 3 People in the area believe the project will be a success.
_____ 4 Building new roads and railways will help to create trade between countries.

5 Work with a partner. Read the sentences from the video. What do you think the words and phrases in bold mean?

WORKING OUT MEANING FROM CONTEXT

1 Five years ago, there was almost nothing here. All of this has been built **from scratch**.
2 Build the roads and rail links out into the regions' developing countries and the trade will follow, **so the theory goes**.
3 This is very much the image of the modern Silk Road the Chinese government wants to **project**.

DISCUSSION

6 Work with a partner and answer the questions.

1 Will international trade increase in the future? Why? / Why not?
2 What recent large infrastructure projects (a new airport, a new stadium, etc.) have there been in your country?

READING 1

PREPARING TO READ

UNDERSTANDING
KEY VOCABULARY

1 **Read the sentences and write the words in bold next to the definitions.**

1 The countries with the strongest economies play the most **dominant** role in globalization.

2 My country experienced high **inflation** last year. Now things like food, housing and transport are much more expensive.

3 Nothing at that shop is sold at a **discount** – it's very expensive.

4 The shipping company has a **reputation** for thorough and on-time delivery. Customers have been very happy with their work.

5 Besides the excellent food at that restaurant, another **selling point** is the beautiful traditional Japanese art and furniture.

6 The corporation is a **multinational** organization with offices in Asia, Europe and Africa.

7 We can't repair the computers until our **supplier** sends us the special parts that we need to do it.

8 I usually buy fruit from local farmers to support the **domestic** economy.

a _____ (adj) relating to a person's own country

b _____ (adj) more powerful or noticeable than anything else of the same type

c _____ (adj) a reduction in the usual price

d _____ (n) the general opinion that people have about someone or something based on their behaviour in the past

e _____ (n) a person or company that provides goods of a particular kind

f _____ (n) a continuing rise in prices in an economy

g _____ (adj) operating in different countries

h _____ (n) a feature that persuades people to buy a product

SKILLS

Making predictions from a text type

Different text types, such as essays, articles and blogs, have different characteristics. Some will be more suitable for academic study than others. Before reading a text, you can make predictions about the information and the style of the writing. The source, title and any visuals can help you predict the content.

2 You are going to read a blog post. Before reading, which of the statements do you think will be true?

1 The style will be informal.
2 The contents will be appropriate for an academic essay.
3 The writer will give his or her personal opinions.
4 The information will be up-to-date.

3 Read the blog and check your predictions. Find examples to support your ideas.

IKEA'S GLOBAL SUCCESS

1 In this entry to my blog series about successful **multinational** companies, I will check out the furniture chain IKEA. IKEA has been the world's **dominant** furniture chain since 2008, according to *Forbes* magazine.

2 Swedish entrepreneur Ingvar Kamprad was only 17 years old when he started the company in 1943. These days, the chain has about 460 stores selling appliances[1], furniture and other household[2] items in over 61 countries around the world. So how have they managed to become such a global hit? Well, to me it seems that three features of the chain stand out: their dedication to research, their affordable prices and their eco-friendly[3] **reputation**.

3 The executives at IKEA have long understood the need to research other markets in order to succeed globally. The company is constantly conducting research on how people use their furniture and what they are looking for. They recently conducted research in eight cities worldwide. This is how they learned, for example, that Korean customers want a special *kimchi*[4] refrigerator.

4 But in order to sell at **discount** prices, they need to make and sell a lot of the same thing to keep costs low. This way, they can get low prices from **suppliers**, and charge super-low prices to their customers. As a result, they can keep their prices economical even during periods of **inflation**. This is why they will show the same products in different ways in their stores, depending on the local culture. A British bedroom display might have a British flag bedspread on it, whereas one in Tokyo may have a traditional mat on the floor. In China, IKEA's fastest-growing market, **domestic** manufacturers make most of the products they sell in order to keep transport costs low.

5 A final **selling point** for many customers is the image of the company. They sell their furniture in flat boxes which use less space and paper and are easier to transport. A company representative recently said that they are working on creating new products out of materials we currently throw away, such as recycled plastic and foil. In some markets, they plan to market an electric bicycle, and in Seoul, they recently planted a tree to celebrate the opening of a new store.

6 Next week, I'll look at other multinational companies which specialize in household goods and automobile production.

[1]**appliances** (n) devices, usually electrical, that are used in the home
[2]**household** (adj) related to people homes
[3]**eco-friendly** (adj) designed to do the least possible damage to the environment
[4]**kimchi** (n) a traditional Korean vegetable dish

WHILE READING

4 Answer the questions with information from the blog.

1 According to the introduction, why has the blogger written this blog entry about IKEA?

2 How might a display in a Japanese IKEA be different from one in the UK?

3 Why does the writer think that IKEA's shipping packaging is eco-friendly?

4 What does the writer plan to write about soon?

5 Read the blog again. Write *T* (true), *F* (false), or *DNS* (does not say) next to the statements. Correct the false statements.

_____ 1 IKEA's founder is from Sweden.

_____ 2 The author identifies three main characteristics of the chain which has made it globally successful.

_____ 3 IKEA executives have only recently wanted to understand new markets.

_____ 4 IKEA has stores in China.

_____ 5 Some IKEA products use recycled glass.

_____ 6 IKEA has plans to sell electric bicycles in all their markets.

6 The blog author uses some informal language. Match informal words and phrases to formal words. Use the context to help you.

1 check out   a a big success
2 super-low   b investigate
3 a hit   c very inexpensive

READING BETWEEN THE LINES

7 Work with a partner. Discuss the questions.

1 Do you think the author is impressed by the age at which Ingvar Kamprad started his own company? Why / Why not?

2 Why does IKEA present products differently in different countries?

3 Why did IKEA decide to plant a tree to celebrate the opening of a new store in Seoul?

DISCUSSION

8 Work with a partner. Discuss the questions.

1 Ikea produces furniture which you have to build yourself. Is this something you like doing? Why / Why not?

2 How important is the presentation of products in a shop?

READING 2

PREPARING TO READ

1 Read the definitions and complete the text with the words in bold.

> **consumption** (n) the amount of something that someone uses, eats or drinks
> **convenience** (n) the state of being suitable for your purposes causing no difficulty
> **ensure** (v) to make certain that something is done or happens
> **experiment** (v) to try a new way of doing something
> **increase** (v) to become larger or greater
> **influence** (n) the power to have an effect on people or things, or someone or something that is able to do this
> **relatively** (adv) quite good, bad, etc. in comparison with other similar things or with what you expect
> **specialty** (n) a product that a place is especially known for

Many shoppers have switched to ordering groceries online because of its ⁽¹⁾_____ . Now they don't leave their homes to buy food. Others, however, prefer to see the food before they buy it to ⁽²⁾_____ that the food is fresh. Recently, the popularity of cooking programmes on television has had a big ⁽³⁾_____ on the ingredients that people use. People want to cook with foods they see on TV.

People sometimes reduce their ⁽⁴⁾_____ of certain foods when those foods become more expensive. For example, if bad weather affects the supply of some fruits or vegetables, it can cause their prices to ⁽⁵⁾_____.

People who travel a lot tend to be ⁽⁶⁾_____ familiar with international food compared to people who don't. Some travellers like to eat familiar food, but others prefer to ⁽⁷⁾_____ with unfamiliar dishes. In Iceland, we tried a bread that is baked in the ground near a hot spring. It's a local ⁽⁸⁾_____.

Topic sentences

Good paragraphs in formal writing usually start with *topic sentences*. These tell you the subject of the paragraph. After the topic sentence you can usually make a prediction about what information will follow. By reading the first sentence of each paragraph in a text, you can often identify which paragraph to look at if you need some specific information.

2 You are going to read an essay about eating habits in Italy.

Read the topic sentences of paragraphs 1–5 and underline the key words. The first one has been done for you. Then, compare with a partner. Did you choose the same words?

Topic Sentence	Detail in the paragraph
1 <u>Globalization</u> is <u>causing</u> a lot of <u>change</u> in <u>international culture</u>, from <u>TV shows</u> we watch to the <u>clothes</u> we wear.	a Indian, Chinese and Japanese food have all become especially popular.
2 In Italy, changing trends have affected the preparation of food.	b These chains are often foreign, and their numbers have increased enormously.
3 Italians' food tastes have changed because of globalization.	c Its influence can be seen as both positive and negative.
4 A third major change in Italy's food culture has been the rise of large restaurant chains.	d In a recent survey in Japan, Brazil and Canada, 72% of people said globalization had improved their eating habits.
5 In summary, globalization has had a significant effect on the way that Italians eat.	e Until recently, pasta – basic Italian food – would have been made by people in their local area.

3 Now match the topic sentences with the correct details a–e from the text. Skim read the essay to check your answers.

WHILE READING

READING FOR MAIN IDEAS

4 Read the essay again and underline the key ideas in each paragraph. Remember that the topic sentence and last line of each paragraph is key when trying to understand the general idea of a paragraph. Using your underlined words, write one or two sentences which summarize each paragraph.

1 _____
2 _____
3 _____
4 _____
5 _____

5 Work with a partner, and discuss the following questions. Try to do this without looking back at the text.

1 How has globalization affected food around the world?
2 How have changing trends affected food preparation in Italy?
3 How have food tastes changed in Italy?
4 Are food chains popular in Italy? Why / Why not?

CHANGING EATING HABITS IN ITALY

1 Globalization is causing a lot of change in international culture, from the TV shows we watch to the clothes we wear. One major area which has been affected by globalization is food culture. In a recent survey taken in Japan, Brazil and Canada, 72% of people said that globalization had improved their eating habits. It seems clear that globalization has significantly affected food consumption in most parts of the world, but one country whose food has a long history of being 'globalized' is Italy. If you walk down any main street in any major world city, you will find at least one Italian restaurant. Furthermore, Italy has seen changes in its own eating habits due to influence from other countries. This influence, which is a result of the broader trend of globalization, has had both advantages and disadvantages.

2 In Italy, changing trends have affected the preparation of food. Italian families have always taken a lot of pride in preparing food. Until recently, pasta – a basic Italian food – would have been made by people in their local area. Families would also have made the sauces to eat with the pasta at home. People no longer spend so much time preparing their meals. Indeed, frozen or take-out Italian meals have become very popular in Italy. Furthermore, dried pasta is now mass-produced[1] and is sold relatively cheaply in supermarkets. Ready-made pasta sauces are also increasingly popular – sales have doubled in the last five years, according to one manufacturer. This has added to the convenience of making meals, but has diminished[2] a cultural tradition.

3 Italians' food tastes have changed because of globalization. People are travelling more, being exposed to other cultures more, and reading about and seeing foreign ingredients and recipes on the internet and social media. Immigrants to Italy bring their food traditions with them. It used to be that people's opportunities to experiment with foreign food were very limited, since only pizza and pasta were available in the local town square. Now they can eat at restaurants with foreign cuisine[3] and buy foreign food in shops. Indian, Chinese and Japanese food have all become especially popular. While this trend is more common in urban areas such as Rome, Milan and Venice, many smaller towns are also experiencing similar changes. Many Italians would say that this has been a positive change, but others worry that they are losing their sense of nationality as foreign food becomes more common.

4 A third major change in Italy's food culture has been the rise of large restaurant chains. These chains are often foreign, and their numbers have increased enormously in recent years. Many people like the convenience of fast food. Some Italians, however, feel that this has resulted in the destruction of local and national specialties. In 1986, a famous fast-food chain opened a restaurant in a historic Rome neighbourhood. Many unhappy people responded by joining the 'Slow Food' movement. This movement encourages people to eat healthy, locally sourced food.

5 In summary, globalization has had a significant effect on the way that Italians eat. Its influence can be seen as both positive and negative. Convenience foods have replaced many of the traditional home-cooked meals, and the availability of foreign foods and international chains has greatly increased. Italians no longer have to rely on food which is produced locally. While some people welcome this extra choice, others fear the damage it may cause to Italian traditions, culture and local businesses. On the other hand, the great popularity of Italian food worldwide will ensure this great cuisine never disappears.

[1]**mass-produced** (adj) made in large amounts, using machinery in a factory

[2]**diminished** (v) made smaller; decreased

[3]**cuisine** (n) style of cooking

READING BETWEEN THE LINES

6 Work with a partner. Choose the best answer for each question.

1 What types of readers is this essay meant to appeal to?
People who *have a general interest / are experts* in Italian food.
2 What do you think is the author's main intention?
To say that globalization has had a *largely positive impact on /
fundamentally changed* Italian food.

DISCUSSION

7 Work with a partner and answer the questions below.

1 Do you prefer going to foreign food restaurants or restaurants
which serve local dishes?
2 Do you think chain restaurants have a positive or negative impact
on society? Why?

WRITING

8 What advantages and disadvantages has globalization had on our
eating habits? Write 150–200 words.

⊙ LANGUAGE DEVELOPMENT

ACADEMIC ALTERNATIVES TO PHRASAL VERBS

VOCABULARY

When writing essays, it is important to use language which is more formal than you
would use when speaking or writing informal pieces.

Phrasal verbs, which usually consist of a main verb followed by a particle (e.g. *up, on*),
are less common in academic writing than in informal writing.

In academic writing, phrasal verbs can often be replaced by a single word.

1 Match the phrasal verbs to the academic verbs.

1	go on	a	increase
2	go up	b	continue
3	turn down	c	study
4	look into	d	confuse
5	use up	e	remove
6	mix up	f	refuse
7	leave out	g	exclude
8	take away	h	exhaust

2 Read the article below and highlight the phrasal verbs used.

The rate of globalization is only set to go up even further in the future. Multinational companies will go on to expand further and use up every possibility they can. This provides an excellent opportunity for people to work and live abroad. However, the process involved in doing this must be looked into carefully beforehand. Many people are turned down for a visa because they are often mixed up about the entry requirements. Some critics believe that current requirements for some countries are too strict and should be taken away. For example, in some countries, if you do not have the right qualifications, you could be left out of the selection process.

3 Make the article more formal by replacing these phrasal verbs with an academic verb in the correct form from Exercise 1.

GLOBALIZATION VOCABULARY

1 Match the words in the box below with the correct definitions (a–f).

discount (n)   domestic (adj)   inflation (n)   monopoly (n)
multinational (adj)   outlet (n)

a a general, continuous increase in price
b an organization or group that has complete control of something, especially in the area of business
c a reduction in the usual price
d relating to or within a person's own country
e a shop that is one of many owned by a particular company
f producing and selling goods in several different countries

2 It is a good idea to learn all forms of a new word. Complete the table. Use a dictionary to help you. Then write your own sentences using each of these words.

Noun	Adjective	Verb
consumption	consumable	*consume*
discount		
	multinational	
inflation		
outlet		
monopoly		
	domestic*	

*domestic *as a business term*

WRITING

CRITICAL THINKING

At the end of this unit, you are going to write an explanatory essay. Look at this unit's writing task below.

How has globalization changed your country?

Evaluating supporting examples

In academic writing, you need to justify and give supporting examples to any statements or opinions that you write to show that they are true. It is important to only use supporting examples which are relevant and appropriate for the point which you are making. In order to do this, you need to evaluate the examples properly.

APPLY

1 Read these statements. What examples are given in Reading 2 that can support them?

1 Italians pride themselves on the making and preparation of food.
2 People's opportunity to experiment with foreign food was very limited.
3 People no longer spend so much time preparing their meals.
4 Italians worry that they are losing their sense of nationality.
5 Globalization has become such a significant influence.

ANALYZE

2 Think of an aspect of globalization that you would like to write about in the Writing task. This can be about food, clothing, entertainment, holidays, language, technology or other aspects of globalization. Write this idea in the middle of the ideas map below, and add any supporting examples which you can think of.

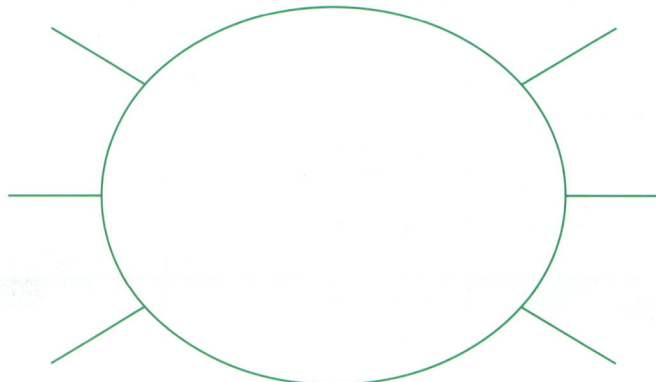

Using tables and diagrams
Tables and diagrams can often help you organize information that you can use to support your ideas in an essay.

3 Complete the table below with the best three supporting examples from the ideas map in Exercise 2. It should follow the format of a body paragraph in an essay on the topic you chose in Exercise 2.

Topic:
Supporting example 1:
Supporting example 2:
Supporting example 3:
Concluding sentence:

GRAMMAR FOR WRITING

NOUN PHRASES

A noun phrase is a group of words in a sentence that together behave as a noun.
Noun phrases can be made by combining nouns with:
- other nouns: *foreign suppliers*
- relative clauses: *a product **which** is sold locally*
- prepositional phrases: *manufacturing **in** Sweden*
- adjectives: *the **dominant** market*

In academic writing, many noun phrases are created by joining two nouns with *of*.
These common phrases with *of* are used to talk about quantity: *a range of*

1 Match one of the sentences below to one of the grammar structures (a–d) in the box.

> a) noun + prepositional phrase   b) adjective + noun
> c) noun + noun   d) noun phrase + relative clause

1 The local specialty is my favourite.
2 World cuisine is sold here.
3 Globalization is a change which is unstoppable.
4 Production in this town is increasing.

2 Rearrange the words to make noun phrases.

1 range / a / exports / of
2 impact / chains / multinational / the / of
3 an / of / international / group / entrepreneurs
4 different / the / cultures / mixture / of

3 Now create your own noun phrases by using the four different ways of combining nouns in Exercise 1.

TIME PHRASES

GRAMMAR

In academic writing, it is helpful to use different phrases to describe the time in which something happened. You can also use these phrases to clarify whether events occurred in the past or are happening now. Sometimes you need to be specific. Other times, you can be more general.

Very specific: *Ingvar Kamprad started the company* **in 1943**.

More general: **In recent years**, *foreign food has become more popular in Italy.*

However, it is important you use the correct tense with these time phrases.

For a specific time in the past you need to use the past simple.

1 Put the time phrases below in the correct part of the table, according to the period of time they refer to.

> around fifty years ago   at the present time   currently
> historically   in recent years   formerly
> in the past   in the 1950s   nowadays   these days
> several years ago   in the eighteenth century   presently

general past time	specific past time	present

2 Complete the following student essay with the correct time phrases. In some cases, more than one answer is possible.

a) _____ , more and more people are being adventurous with their food choices. b) _____ , people have been experimenting with new foods, and this is partly due to globalization. c) _____ people are travelling more and have the opportunity to taste authentic food from other countries. d) _____ , however, this was certainly not the case and the majority of people just ate the local food.

ACADEMIC WRITING SKILLS

ESSAY STRUCTURE

Although there are different types of academic essays, the overall structure and principles tend to be the same. Academic essays start with an *introductory paragraph*, followed by *body paragraphs* and end with a *concluding paragraph*.

Introductory paragraph

A strong introductory paragraph is very important when writing an academic essay, as it the first impression the reader gets of your work. A good introduction presents the topic of your essay and explains what the essay is about / your opinion (this is called a thesis statement). As the introductory paragraph sets the tone for the rest of the essay it is important that particular attention is given to accuracy, particularly in relation to spelling and grammar.

Some academic essays start with a *hook* – an interesting fact or statement, a surprising statistic, a quotation or question to get the reader's attention.

Body paragraphs

These develop the main ideas outlined in the introduction and include relevant evidence and supporting information.

Concluding paragraph

The last paragraph presents a restatement of the thesis of the essay and ends with the conclusions, recommendations or predictions of the writer.

SKILLS

1 Read the example essay below. Structure the essay by putting the paragraphs in the correct order. Use the guidance from page 29 to help you.

Is globalization a positive or negative development? Discuss.

Paragraph A

However, there are also drawbacks. The increased movement of people across borders means that diseases can spread more quickly than before. Also, our economies are more linked, which means that when one country experiences a financial crisis, it can impact many others. Finally, large international corporations can create unfair competition for local businesses.

Paragraph B

When did globalization begin? Historians might suggest that it was when Christopher Columbus made his voyages to the Americas in the 1490s. For most of us, however, we tend to think of it as a more modern phenomenon connected with the rise of the worldwide web. In any case, when it comes to the question of whether globalization is beneficial or not, it is complicated. A review of some of the features of globalization suggests that it has had both pros and cons.

Paragraph C

Clearly there are advantages and disadvantages to globalization. How to balance this is a debate that has been going on for some time. One thing seems clear, however: we citizens are more connected than ever before. We can probably predict that this will not change.

Paragraph D

The international spread of information, technology, products and ideas has enriched our lives in many ways. When something new is invented far away, we can get it at home. Governments can share ideas with each other to keep us all safer. Also, we can enjoy each others' cultures more than ever before by experiencing new food and different types of entertainment.

Order the paragraphs by putting the letters in the correct order

1 _____

2 _____

3 _____

4 _____

Discuss with a partner. Which parts of each paragraph helped you structure the essay correctly?

WRITING AN EFFECTIVE THESIS STATEMENT IN THE INTRODUCTION

SKILLS

A **thesis statement** in an academic essay is usually found **at the very end of the introductory paragraph**. It explains what the entire essay will be about, and it expresses a writer's point of view. With a good thesis statement, readers can guess what the rest of the essay might look like.

A thesis statement should sound like an opinion. It should not sound like a fact, a question, a description of what the essay will contain, or a general idea which everyone agrees on.

Essay topic	Possible thesis statement
The effects of globalization	*Globalization has brought us both advantages and disadvantages, but the benefits have been far greater than the drawbacks.*

From this thesis statement the reader can understand **what** the writer will discuss (advantages and disadvantages of globalization) and what the writer's overall opinion is (the benefits of globalization have been far greater than the drawbacks).

Remember to use formal language in your thesis statement:

This essay will discuss **not** *I will* **talk about** ...

2 Below are some examples of thesis statements. From each statement the reader should be able to understand what the essay question was. Discuss with a partner what you think the question was for each of these statements.

a Chain stores can have a negative impact on the local high street. This essay will discuss the problems they can cause and offer some solutions.

b Around the world, obesity is becoming an increasing problem. This is because eating habits have changed due to fast food and globalization.

c Globalization has had both a positive and negative effect on my local area. In the following essay both sides of the argument will be discussed.

3 Now look at the essay questions below and write a thesis statement for each.

a Globalization is a threat to the local culture of individual countries. To what extent do you agree?

b Globalization has meant that many students now choose to study abroad. What are the positive and negative effects of this trend?

c How do you think globalization will have changed in fifty years? Will its effects have increased or decreased around the world?

WRITING TASK

How has globalization changed your country?

STRUCTURE & PLAN

1 Look at page 29 again to remind yourself of how to structure an academic essay.

2 Now look at Reading 2 and underline the following:

Introduction
a a statement which introduces the topic
b the hook
c the thesis statement

Main Body
d supporting argument + one detail (paragraph 2)
e supporting argument + one detail (paragraph 3)
f supporting argument + one detail (paragraph 4)

Conclusion
g the summary statement
h a restatement of the thesis
i a final thought / prediction

International shops and restaurants in Chonburi, Thailand

3 Before you start to write, it is important to write some notes about what you are going to include in each paragraph. Use the table below to help you.

	Remember to include	Notes
Paragraph 1 **Introduction**	a statement to introduce the topic a hook (optional) a thesis statement	
Paragraph 2 **Body paragraphs**	your supporting argument with examples / details	
Paragraph 3 **Body paragraphs**	your supporting argument with examples / details	
Paragraph 4 **Body paragraphs**	your supporting argument with examples / details	
Paragraph 5 **Conclusion**	a summary statement a restatement of the thesis a final thought, recommendation or prediction	

4 Refer to the Task checklist on page 34 as you prepare your essay.

WRITE A FIRST DRAFT

5 Write the first draft of your essay. Use your essay plan to structure your essay.

Include an introductory paragraph, a thesis statement, three body paragraphs with supporting ideas and a concluding paragraph with a final thought, recommendation or prediction. Write 350–400 words.

REVISE

6 Use the Task checklist to review your essay for content and structure.

TASK CHECKLIST	✔
Did you structure your essay?	
Does the introductory paragraph have a clear thesis statement?	
Does each paragraph focus on the information it is supposed to?	
Did you include topic sentences for each paragraph?	
Did you include evidence to support your topic sentences?	
Is there a concluding paragraph with a concluding thought, recommendation or prediction?	

7 Make any necessary changes to your essay.

EDIT

8 Use the Language checklist to edit your essay for language errors.

LANGUAGE CHECKLIST	✔
Do the words in any noun phrases appear in the right order?	
Did you use time phrases correctly?	
Did you use academic verbs instead of phrasal verbs where possible?	
Did you spell academic verbs correctly?	

9 Make any necessary changes to your essay.

OBJECTIVES REVIEW

1 Check your learning objectives for this unit. Write *3*, *2* or *1* for each objective.

3 = very well   2 = well   1 = not so well

I can ...

watch and understand a video about China's plans to revive the Silk Road trade routes. _____

make predictions from a text type. _____

recognize topic sentences. _____

evaluate supporting examples. _____

use tables and diagrams. _____

use noun phrases. _____

use time phrases. _____

use correct essay structure. _____

write an effective thesis statement. _____

write an explanatory essay. _____

2 Use the *Unlock* Digital Workbook for more practice with this unit's learning objectives.

UNLOCK
DIGITAL
WORKBOOK

WORDLIST

confuse (v) ⊙
consumption (n) ⊙
continue (v) ⊙
convenience (n) ⊙
discount (n) ⊙
domestic (adj)
dominant (adj)
ensure (v) ⊙
exclude (v) ⊙

exhaust (v) ⊙
experiment (v) ⊙
increase (v) ⊙
inflation (n) ⊙
influence (n) ⊙
monopoly (n) ⊙
multinational (adj)
outlet (n) ⊙

refuse (v) ⊙
relatively (adv)
remove (v) ⊙
reputation (n) ⊙
selling point (n)
specialty (n) ⊙
study (v) ⊙
supplier (n) ⊙

⊙ = high-frequency words in the Cambridge Academic Corpus

EDUCATION

LEARNING OBJECTIVES

Watch and listen
Watch and understand a video about global literacy campaigns.

Reading skill
Make inferences.

Critical thinking
Analyze similarities and differences; use a Venn diagram to plan a comparison-contrast essay.

Grammar
Use transitions to show comparison and contrast; use adverb clauses of contrast.

Academic writing skill
Avoid run-on sentences and comma splices; write a comparison and contrast essay.

Writing task
Write a comparison and contrast essay.

UNL⊘CK YOUR KNOWLEDGE

Work with a partner. Discuss the questions.

1 Look at the photo. What do you think the people are studying?

2 What do you think of the education system in your country? What do you think works well and what could be improved?

3 How do you think your education system could become more modernized and useful for today's generation? Think about new subjects, and technology for the classroom.

4 At what age can students leave school in your country? What type of exams do you have to take before you leave school?

WATCH AND LISTEN

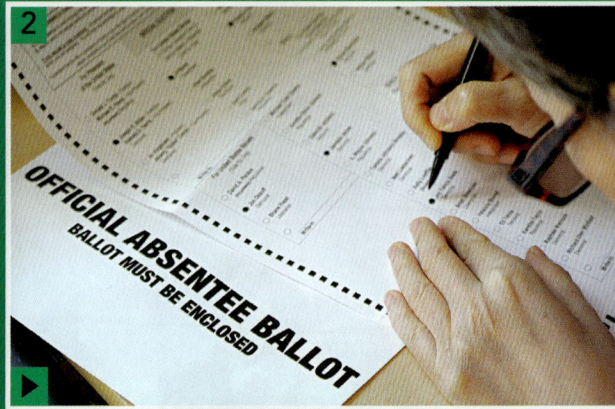

PREPARING TO WATCH

ACTIVATING YOUR KNOWLEDGE

1 Work with a partner and answer the questions.

1 How do you think your life would be different if you were unable to read or write?

2 Do you think it is harder to learn new things as you get older? Why / Why not?

PREDICTING CONTENT USING VISUALS

2 Look at the photos from the video. Discuss the questions with a partner.

1 Where do you think Photo 1 was taken? Describe the pupils.

2 How do Photos 2, 3 and 4 show that being able to read and write is necessary for our daily life?

GLOSSARY

illiteracy (n) a lack of the ability to read and write

disadvantaged (adj) not having the standard of living conditions, education, etc. that most people have

drop out (phr v) to not do something that you were going to do (e.g. not finish a course)

stigma (n) a strong feeling of disapproval that most people in a society have about something, especially when this is unfair

turn to sth (phr v) to start to do something bad, especially when unhappy

WHILE WATCHING

UNDERSTANDING MAIN IDEAS

3 ▶ Watch the video and answer the questions.

1 What are the main aims of Project Literacy?

2 Who does Idris Elba speak about and why?

3 What is the impact on children whose parents cannot read or write?

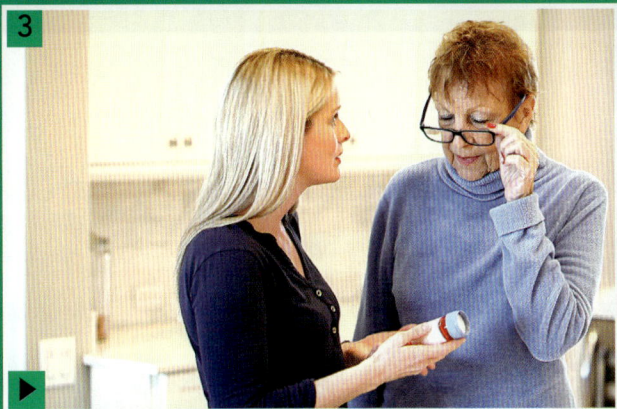

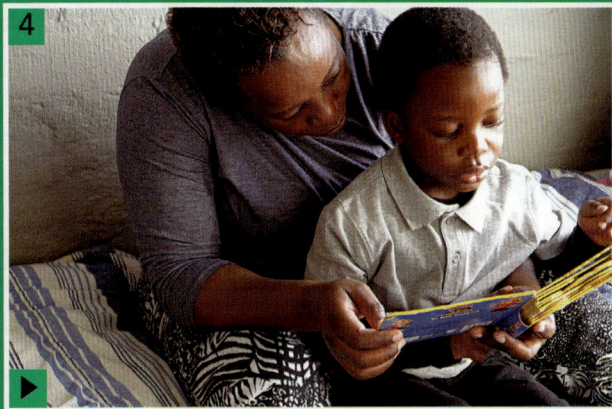

4 ▶ **Watch again. Which of the summaries below best describes the main message in the video?**

SUMMARIZING

1 Illiteracy affects people of all ages all over the world. However, it is most common in older women, particularly in India. Recently, however, schools have been set up in India to tackle this problem.

2 Illiteracy affects people of all ages all over the world. For older generations, not being able to read and write can mean feeling excluded from society. This is just one of the issues Project Literacy aims to tackle.

3 The aim of Project Literacy is to make sure that the older generation is able to read and write well. This will then ensure that they encourage their children to do the same.

5 Answer the questions.

MAKING INFERENCES

1 Why were the Indian women in the video so happy to be at school?

2 Why are many adults afraid to admit they can't read or write?

3 Why did they give thumb prints at the bank?

DISCUSSION

6 Work with a partner and answer the questions. Give reasons for your answers.

1 What could governments around the world do to tackle the issue of illiteracy?

2 What could be done in your own country to solve this problem?

READING 1

PREPARING TO READ

1 You are going to read an essay with the title *A Traditional Degree Versus a Degree Apprenticeship*. Look at the photos. Which photo shows a *traditional degree* course and which a *degree apprenticeship*? What do you think is the main difference between the two types of course?

2 Work with a partner and tick (✔) the phrases you think will be mentioned in connection with a traditional degree, a degree apprenticeship or both. Give reasons to support your choices.

	Traditional degree	Degree apprenticeship	Both
1 earn as they learn		✔	
2 student experience			
3 lectures and seminars			
4 joining clubs or societies			
5 holiday time			
6 wide range of career choices			

3 Match the words in the box to their meaning. Compare your
answers in pairs or groups.

> **employability** (n)   **pursue** (v)   **community** (n)   **peer** (n)
> **deadline** (n)   **regard** (v)   **in-depth** (adj)   **aspect** (n)

1 have respect for someone for something
2 the abilities and skills that allow someone to be employed
3 try and achieve something
4 one part of something
5 a group of people who have something in common or who live in
   the same place
6 someone of the same age, ability or position within the same
   group
7 the time by which something needs to be completed
8 in a very detailed and careful way

4 Complete the questions with the correct form of a word from
Exercise 3. There is one word you will not use. Then discuss the
questions in groups. Give reasons to support your ideas.

1 How do you develop your _____ ?
2 Why do some students find _____ their dream job difficult
   after they graduate?
3 How important is it for university students to feel part of a
   _____ ? Why / Why not?
4 Are you good at meeting _____ both at work and in study?
   Why / Why not?
5 What qualities do you think are _____ as important by an
   employer?
6 What _____ of school or university life do students most
   enjoy?
7 Which subject or area of work would you like to explore
   _____ ?

UNIVERSITY COURSES:

A TRADITIONAL DEGREE VS A DEGREE APPRENTICESHIP

1 Traditional university degrees have been valued for hundreds of years. A university education allows graduates to make better choices by increasing job opportunities for a broad range of careers. Research shows that men with a university education can earn salaries of around 8% more than their **peers** and for graduate women the gap is even bigger at 28%. It is not surprising, therefore, that university is the most popular higher education option with nearly eight hundred thousand school-leavers starting a degree course in 2023. However, even though a traditional degree is extremely beneficial, it can still be extremely challenging for graduates to find a job due to a lack of work experience. Degree apprenticeships, which were introduced in the UK in 2015, are realistic alternatives to gaining a degree qualification, particularly with school-leavers who want to 'earn as they learn'. Whilst both degrees have the same qualification level, they differ significantly in terms of the student experience and **employability**, and it is essential for school-leavers to carefully consider these differences before choosing which option to **pursue**.

2 Student life will be different for an apprentice compared to other forms of higher education. Although degree apprentices will experience certain **aspects** of campus life, they will not share the traditional experience of students who are studying at university full-time. For example, rather than spend around 30 hours per week on campus attending lectures and seminars and completing assignments in their own time, apprentices spend this time 'on the job' learning workplace skills with just 20% set aside for university. Of course, this means they also have less free time to take part in [1]extra-curricular activities, like joining clubs or societies. Holiday time is also markedly different in that full-time students get over three months holiday annually at the end of term or semester. Conversely, apprentices, as they are employees as well as students, receive just four or five weeks. Therefore, whilst apprentices gain real-life work experience while earning a wage, they not only have to balance working and studying at the same time but may also feel excluded from the student **community**.

3 Research suggests that one of the main advantages graduate apprentices have over their peers is that they learn key workplace skills. During their apprenticeship students will attend meetings and meet **deadlines**. They will build valuable relationships with colleagues at many different levels and may even communicate with external [2]stakeholders like customers. These [3]'soft skills', for example, teamwork and time-management, will help graduate apprentices achieve success throughout their working lives. However, degree apprenticeships tend to be vocational, and whilst they are not limited to trades or engineering, they do not currently offer the enormous choice of traditional university degrees. In addition, although apprentices can quit, if they choose not to continue in their chosen industry, they may find they have limited qualifications to transfer to another employer.

4 To conclude, traditional degrees and degree apprenticeships are both excellent choices for school-leavers and are well **regarded** by employers, but they differ in significant ways. Degree apprenticeships do not give students the same 'traditional' student experience nor the wide range of career choices which the open nature of a traditional degree provides. On the other hand, degree apprenticeships provide **in-depth** workplace experience and commercial skills whilst allowing students to earn a salary as they study. As the number of UK employers offering degree apprenticeship continues to rise, it will be interesting to see whether more and more school leavers choose this option over the traditional route.

---

[1]**extra-curricular** (adj) an extra activity that is not normally part of a course.
[2]**stakeholder** (n) a person such as a customer, employee, or citizen who is involved in a company.
[3]**soft skills** (n) people's ability to communicate and work well together

WHILE READING

READING FOR
MAIN IDEAS

5 Read the essay. Which option (1–3) best expresses the main idea?

1 A traditional university degree is the most popular choice among school leavers but with the introduction of the degree apprenticeship in 2015 that may change in the future.

2 The two courses are delivered in very different ways with degree apprentices receiving 'on-the-job' training rather than being fully immersed in the 'traditional' student life.

3 A degree apprenticeship may improve a graduate's ability to find a job because he/she can gain important workplace experience and learn key skills, such as effective time management.

READING FOR
DETAIL

6 Read the essay again. For each sentence choose the correct option. Underline in the essay where you found the answer.

1 Research has found that *men / both men and women* who have a degree qualification earn higher salaries.

2 Degree apprentices are in the workplace for *up to 30 hours / about one day* a week.

3 Traditional degree courses offer *fewer vocational / a wider range of* courses than degree apprenticeships.

READING BETWEEN THE LINES

SKILLS

Inferences

Sometimes writers suggest the meaning of something without saying it directly. Being able to read this **inferred meaning** (as well as the literal meaning of the words) is a useful skill. Practise using logic to work out the real meaning of the words you read.

MAKING
INFERENCES

7 Work with a partner. Discuss the questions.

1 Why does the writer refer to the number of school leavers who decide to do a traditional degree as 'not surprising'?

2 Overall, do you think the writer favours degree apprenticeships?

DISCUSSION

8 Discuss the following question in pairs or small groups.

What skills are necessary for each type of degree?

WRITING

9 Write a paragraph of about 100 words explaining if you would prefer to study a traditional degree or a degree apprenticeship.

READING 2

PREPARING TO READ

1 You are going to read an article about distance and face-to-face learning. Before you read, match the collocations to their meanings.

1 core principles   a recent trend
2 credible alternative   b important distinction
3 distance learning   c an academic qualification obtained from online instruction
4 modern phenomenon   d key values
5 online degree   e general education from online instruction
6 significant difference   f online course
7 technological advances   g reliable substitute
8 virtual classroom   h developments in technology

2 Complete the sentences and discuss your answers with a partner.

1 One interesting **modern phenomenon** in my country is
_____.

2 A subject which might not work well for **distance learning** is
_____.

3 One advantage of a real classroom over a **virtual classroom** is
_____.

4 One advantage of an **online degree** over a degree which requires attending classes is _____.

5 It's possible that a **credible alternative** to a university education might be _____.

6 Because of **technological advances**, it is now much easier to
_____.

7 One of the **core principles** of many universities is
_____.

8 One **significant difference** between secondary school and university is _____.

3 Look at the statements below. Do you think these statements are *T* (true) or *F* (false)? Correct the false statements.

_____ 1 Distance learning is a new idea.
_____ 2 Distance learning requires good technological access.
_____ 3 Face-to-face learning is better than distance learning.

4 Read the article and check your answers to Exercise 3.

DISTANCE LEARNING VS FACE-TO-FACE LEARNING

1 Although many people think it is a **modern phenomenon**, **distance learning** has been around for at least 200 years in one form or another. Historical examples of long-distance learning include students being sent a series of weekly lessons by mail. The **technological advances** of the past 20 or so years, however, have meant that this form of education is now a **credible alternative** to face-to-face learning. Indeed, 1996 saw the establishment of the world's first 'virtual university' in the United States, showing how far distance learning has come in a relatively short space of time. While it is now possible to obtain a large variety of **online degrees**, which is the best type of education to pursue? A closer examination of this topic reveals that distance and traditional educational instruction have **significant differences** but also some similarities.

2 When comparing the two systems, the most obvious difference lies in the way that instruction is delivered. Distance learning is heavily dependent on technology, particularly the internet. In a face-to-face course, students may only require a computer for the purpose of writing an essay. In comparison, when learning remotely, technology is the principal means of communication. Face-to-face instruction must take place in real time and in one location. Conversely, distance learning can happen at any time and in any location, since the learning is not restricted by geography. The flexibility this provides means that students may be better able to learn at their own pace, but it may also mean that learners have to be well organized and self-disciplined. In other words, they must be more highly motivated in order to do well in distance-learning courses. Finally, with face-to-face learning, the teacher and student have the opportunity to develop a personal relationship. In a **virtual classroom**, by contrast, the teacher may seldom or never actually meet the student. This may make it hard for teachers to understand their students' specific learning needs.

3 Although the nature of the teacher-student relationship may differ in the two methods, they do share the same **core principles**. Just as a teacher is the 'knower' in a classroom, he or she is the one responsible for helping students understand the key sections of an online course. The teacher needs to decide how to best present the material to be learned and in which sequence the topics should be introduced. He or she must also create the assignments for the course and help the students know what resources (textbooks, websites and so on) will best support their learning. Additionally, a teacher needs to provide student feedback in some way. For example, a language teacher in a classroom may be able to correct a student's grammar or pronunciation in the moment, whereas a distance-learning teacher may need to provide written or recorded feedback to be delivered later. In any case, all the usual elements of the teacher's role are necessary, no matter what kind of instruction is being used.

4 It is difficult to state whether one form of learning is better than another, since they are geared towards different learning situations. They are certainly different experiences. Nevertheless, there are strong similarities between the two systems, which can both produce positive results. A student who has the choice should consider the advantages and disadvantages of each method before deciding to take a course.

WHILE READING

5 Write the correct paragraph number (1–4) next to the description.

1 Similarities between the two methods _____

2 General summary and conclusions _____

3 Differences between the methods _____

4 The history and background of the topic _____

6 What does the writer think are the advantages and disadvantages of each type of learning? Complete the tables below.

Distance learning

advantages	disadvantages
Not limited by geography	

Face-to face learning

advantages	disadvantages

READING BETWEEN THE LINES

7 Work with a partner. Answer the questions based on your understanding of the information in the article.

1 Why is the difference that is mentioned in paragraph 2 called 'obvious'?

_____

2 Why can online learning be slightly impersonal?

_____

3 Paragraph 3 states that 'all the usual elements of the teacher's role are necessary' in any kind of instruction. What are these elements?

_____

4 Do you think this author generally approves or disapproves of distance learning? Why?

_____

DISCUSSION

8 Work with a partner. Use ideas from Reading 1 and Reading 2 to discuss the following questions.

1 Have you ever tried to learn something online? What were the advantages and disadvantages of doing this?

2 Which model of learning do you prefer? Why?

⊙ LANGUAGE DEVELOPMENT

EDUCATION VOCABULARY

assignment	campus	degree	dissertation	examination
journal	lecturer	plagiarism	seminar	term	tutor

1 Complete the statements with some of the words from the box. Then circle the option in *italics* to give your own opinion.

1 If a student commits _____ by copying from their sources, or by not acknowledging them, when writing an essay, they *should / should not* be removed from the course immediately.

2 Research papers, known as _____ *should / should not* be available free of charge to students from poorer backgrounds.

3 When you need to pass a formal _____ to get a specific qualification, you should revise *on your own / with peers.*

4 When I am given an _____ to complete, I usually *manage / do not manage* to hand it in on time.

5 I am more *comfortable / less comfortable* attending _____ rather than lectures because you get the opportunity to speak.

2 Complete the sentences with the rest of the words from Exercise 1.

1 As a _____ assumes responsibility for a students' academic and personal welfare, *relationship building* is one of the most important skills they should possess.

2 The academic year is divided into three _____ . In my opinion, these are too long and students should get time off.

3 All university _____ courses should be free of charge for people under the age of 25.

4 Writing a _____ at the end of a degree course, with a word count of 12,000, isn't the best way to assess a student.

5 A university _____ which is all in one place is better than a one which is spread across a city or town.

6 A university _____ should not carry out research during term time, as his/her focus should be on teaching.

ACADEMIC VOCABULARY

3 Match the first part of the sentences (1–9) to the correct ending (a–i). (Use the Glossary on page 38 to help you).

1 More and more school leavers are choosing a degree apprenticeship as an

2 The flexibility offered by distance learning is seen as a

3 Meeting the other students on the course is one beneficial

4 Tutors work with students to help them understand the key

5 Distance learning requires students to have a high level of

6 Distance learning can make it hard for a teacher to understand the

7 Students can often take optional elective classes as well as the

8 1996 saw the creation of the world's first

9 Both degree apprenticeships and traditional degrees are offered

a **virtual** university.

b **significant** benefit by many students.

c **aspect** of a traditional university education.

d **motivation** to succeed.

e **specific** needs a learner has.

f **core** course modules.

g **alternative** to a traditional academic degree course.

h **at university establishments** across the country.

i **principles** of their course.

4 Work in pairs. Choose three words from Exercise 1 and three words from Exercise 3. Then write six questions for your classmates to answer.

Would you like to write a dissertation? What gives you motivation?

WRITING

CRITICAL THINKING

At the end of this unit, you are going to write a comparison and contrast essay. Look at this unit's writing task below.

> Discuss the various similarities and differences between studying a language and studying Mathematics.

1 Look at the two ideas maps below. One is labelled 'Studying a language' and the other 'Studying Mathematics'. Add details according to your experience of studying these subjects.

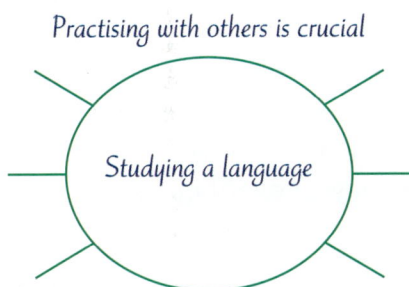

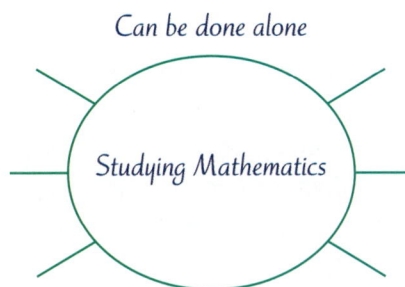

UNDERSTAND

Practising with others is crucial

Studying a language

Can be done alone

Studying Mathematics

Analyzing similarities and differences

In academic discourse, it is often important to compare and contrast information to see the similarities and differences between topics or ideas. A Venn diagram is a very common way of doing this. Use the Venn diagram to discuss the various similarities and differences between studying a language and studying Maths.

SKILLS

2 Write the information from the ideas maps in Exercise 1 into the appropriate parts of the Venn diagram. Try to get at least three pieces of information in each of the three sections. Do more research online to add new information.

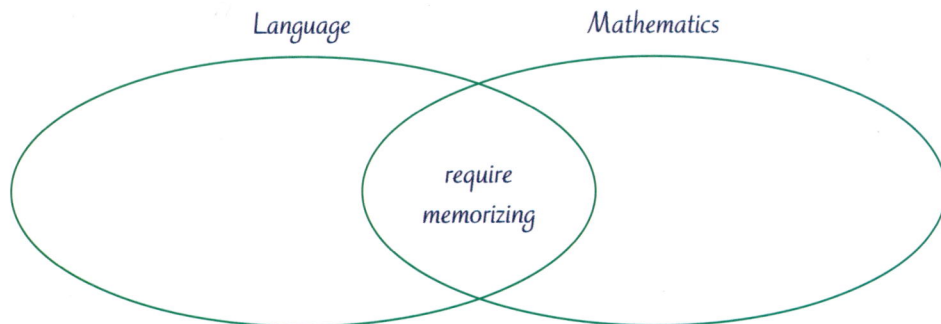

ANALYZE

Language   *Mathematics*

require memorizing

3 Compare your Venn diagram with a partner. Are there any good ideas which you could add to yours?

GRAMMAR FOR WRITING

COMPARISON AND CONTRAST LANGUAGE

Transitions to show comparison and contrast

The ability to **compare** similar ideas or to **contrast** different ideas is an important skill in academic writing.

Students in face-to-face courses see tutors often. <u>*Similarly*</u>*, students in distance-learning courses contact their tutors in online forums often.*

Universities charge high fees for academic subjects. <u>*However*</u>*, colleges charge much less for vocational courses.*

Words such as *however* and *similarly* are called **transition words**. When transition words begin a sentence, they must be followed by a **comma.**

1 Complete the table with transition words or phrases from the box.

> although   compared to   conversely   equally
> however   in contrast   in the same way   nevertheless
> on the other hand   similarly

Comparison words which mean something is **similar**	Contrasting words which mean something is **the opposite**

2 Complete the sentences below using a transition word or phrase from Exercise 1.

1 Traditional degree students spend 30 hours per week on campus attending lectures and seminars, _____ apprentices spend just one day per week at university. (contrast)

2 Traditional degrees are valuable for school leavers as they increase career choices _____ apprenticeships are valued as they provide opportunities for workplace experience. (contrast)

3 Traditional degrees will provide you with useful knowledge for the future, _____ degree apprenticeships will also equip you with the skills you need for the workplace. (similar)

3 In pairs, discuss the topic below. Use a variety of transition words and phrases from the box to help you explain your ideas.

Learning a new language in your home country versus learning a new language abroad

Adverb clauses of contrast

Adverb clauses of contrast are used mainly to contrast two things or ideas.

An adverb clause has a **subject** and a **verb**, but it is not a complete sentence. It begins with the words **while** or **whereas.**

While/Whereas online learning is convenient, face-to-face learning is more interactive.
Online learning is convenient, whereas/while **face-to-face learning is more interactive.**
In sentences expressing contrast, *while* and *whereas* have the same meaning.

As shown in the examples, an adverb clause can come at the **beginning of a sentence** or in the **middle (after the main clause)**. In academic writing, it is more common for adverb clauses of contrast to appear second.

For students who are very academic traditional degrees are a good option, **whereas** *for more practically-minded people the degree apprenticeship is perhaps more suitable.*

Using a comma

Note that if the adverbial clause comes before the main clause, it is followed by a comma. If the adverbial clause comes after the main clause, the comma goes before the adverb clause to emphasize contrast.

Maths can be useful for degrees such as Economics, whereas a language can be necessary for International business.
While studying at university in your hometown can be more economical, studying away from home can give you more independence.

4 Circle the sentence which uses the adverb clause correctly. Pay attention to sentence structure and punctuation.

1 a Graduate men tend to earn around 8% more than non-graduates, whereas graduate women earn just under 30% more.
 b Graduate men tend to earn around 8% more than non-graduates whereas, graduate women earn just under 30% more.

2 a While degree apprentices spend about one day per week on campus. Full-time students are at university for about 30 hours.
 b While degree apprentices spend about one day per week on campus, full-time students are at university for about 30 hours.

3 a Certain students prefer studying online while, others lack motivation.
 b While certain students prefer studying online, others lack motivation.

5 Complete the sentences so that they are true for you. Compare your answers with a partner.

1 Studying English requires _____ , whereas studying science needs _____ .
2 While some students choose to _____ in their free time, I prefer _____ .
3 I study best _____ , while some of my friends prefer to study _____ .

6 Write sentences using these prompts. Try to use the adverbial clause both at the beginning and middle of each sentence. Remember to include the comma in your sentences.

1 university life / school life
2 studying Maths / studying a language
3 lectures / seminars

*I like studying alone, **whereas** my brother prefers to study with his friends.*
***Whereas** my brother prefers to study with his friends, I like studying alone.*

Compare your sentences with a partner. Did you have similar ideas?

ACADEMIC WRITING SKILLS

AVOIDING RUN-ON SENTENCES AND COMMA SPLICES

Run-on sentences and comma splices are common errors that writers must know how to avoid in academic writing. If they are used incorrectly, they can make it difficult for the reader to understand what you mean.

What is a run-on sentence?
A run on sentence is two independent clauses that have not been connected in the right way.

independent clause	independent clause

✗ *Engineering and Business are both popular subjects they both use mathematics.*
✗ *Traditional degrees and degree apprenticeships are both valuable degrees they are highly valued by employers.*

This sentence is incorrect because it is missing a word to link the ideas together such as *and*, *but*, *so*, etc. or the use of punctuation to separate the clauses.

How to avoid run-on sentences

- add a coordinating conjunction, like *and, but* or *so*.

  *Traditional degrees and degree apprenticeships are both valuable degrees, **and** they are highly valued by employers.*

- separate the clauses with a semicolon.

  Traditional degrees and degree apprenticeships are both valuable degrees; they are highly valued by employers.

- separate the clauses with a full stop and make into two sentences.

  Traditional degrees and degree apprenticeships are both valuable degrees. They are highly valued by employers.

What is a comma splice?

A comma splice is two independent clauses connected only with a comma.

missing word / punctuation

✗ *A traditional degree is more popular than a degree apprenticeship, it offers a wider choice of subjects.*

The two independent clauses should instead be linked by a coordinating conjunction or the use of punctuation to separate the clauses.

✔ *A traditional degree is more popular than a degree apprenticeship **because** it offers a wider choice of subjects.*

✔ *A traditional degree is more popular than a degree apprenticeship; it offers a wider choice of subjects.*

How to avoid a comma splice

- add a coordinating conjunction, like *and, but* or *so*.

  A traditional degree is more popular than a degree apprenticeship, and it also offers a wider choice of subjects.

- separate the clauses with a semicolon.

  Traditional degrees are more popular than degree apprenticeships; they also offer a wider choice of subjects.

- separate the clauses with a full stop and make them into two sentences.

  Traditional degrees are more popular than degree apprenticeships. They also offer a wider choice of subjects.

1 Identify the run-on sentences or comma splices in the sentences. Write C (comma splice) or R (run-on sentence). Then correct them.

1 Many students study a second language‸*, and* some students study a third language. __R__

2 Degree apprenticeships are popular among school leavers, they are not as popular as traditional degrees. _____

3 Maths focuses on numbers languages focus on words. _____

4 Distance learning has become very popular you can even earn a degree this way. _____

5 Some students prefer to study academic subjects other students prefer vocational courses. _____

6 All universities charge tuition fees some are more expensive than others. _____

COMPARISON AND CONTRAST ESSAYS

SKILLS

One common way to structure a comparison and contrast essay is to start with a discussion about the differences between the two subjects and then follow with a discussion about the similarities.

Introductory paragraph:

• gives some background on the two subjects of comparison

• provides a thesis statement which explains whether the writer feels that the differences or similarities are more important, or just that they both exist

Body paragraph 1: states the differences between subject 1 and subject 2

Body paragraph 2: states the similarities between subject 1 and subject 2

Concluding paragraph:

• restates the thesis   • ends with a comment showing the writer's opinion

2 Work with a partner. Discuss the questions.

1 In Reading 1, does the thesis statement indicate that the author will emphasize differences between the degree types, similarities between them or that both differences and similarities exist?

2 In Reading 2, does the thesis statement indicate that the author will emphasize the differences of the subjects, the similarities of the subjects or that both differences and similarities exist?

3 In the explanation of comparison and contrast essays which was just presented, the suggested structure of the body paragraphs is that the first discusses differences and the second discusses similarities. Which Reading (1 or 2) follows this structure?

WRITING TASK

Discuss the various similarities and differences between studying a language and studying Mathematics. Write about 350–400 words.

PLAN

1 Look back at the Venn diagram in Critical thinking with your notes on the similarities and differences between studying a language and studying Mathematics. Now take those ideas, plus any new ones you can think of, and create an outline for your essay using the structure below.

	Your notes
Introductory paragraph: (background information, thesis statement) (about 50–100 words)	*Maths and languages are two important subjects which many people choose to study at university. While Maths is….*
Body paragraph 1: (differences) **Try to include at least 3 points** (about 100 words)	*When comparing the two subjects, the most obvious difference….*
Body paragraph 2: (similarities) **Try to include at least 3 points** (about 100 words)	*Although the subjects are very different, they do share some core principles…*
Concluding paragraph: (re-instate your opinion) (about 50–100 words)	

2 Remember you can use an adverb clause with *while* or *whereas* to show contrast for your thesis statement. Look at the thesis statements below, taken from Reading 1 and 2, and underline the adverb clause in each:

Whilst both degrees have the same qualification level, they differ significantly in terms of the student experience … – Reading 1
While it is now possible to obtain a large variety of online degrees, which is the best type of education to pursue? – Reading 2

3 Now write your own thesis statement.

4 Refer to the Task checklist on page 56 as you plan your essay.

WRITE A FIRST DRAFT

5 Write your essay using the outline.

REVISE

6 Use the Task checklist to review your essay for content and structure.

TASK CHECKLIST	✔
Did you give background information and a thesis statement in your introduction?	
Do you have one body paragraph about the differences and another body paragraph about the similarities?	
Did you use examples to strengthen your arguments in the body paragraphs?	
Did you restate the thesis statement and give your opinion in the conclusion?	
Did you write at least 3 differences and 3 similarities?	
Did you check the word count?	

7 Make any necessary changes to your essay.

EDIT

8 Use the Language checklist to edit your essay for language errors.

LANGUAGE CHECKLIST	✔
Did you use comparison and contrast language correctly?	
Did you use adverb clauses to show contrast correctly?	
Did you use a range of academic words?	
Did you use collocations correctly?	
Did you avoid run-on sentences and comma splices?	

9 Make any necessary changes to your essay.

OBJECTIVES REVIEW

1 Check your learning objectives for this unit. Write *3*, *2* or *1* for each objective.

3 = very well   2 = well   1 = not so well

I can …

watch and understand a video about global literacy campaigns.   _____

make inferences and analyze similarities and differences.   _____

use a Venn diagram to plan a comparison-contrast essay.   _____

use transitions to show comparison and contrast.   _____

use adverb clauses of contrast.   _____

avoid run-on sentences and comma splices.   _____

write a comparison and contrast essay.   _____

2 Use the *Unlock* Digital Workbook for more practice with this unit's learning objectives.

UNLOCK
DIGITAL
WORKBOOK

WORDLIST

alternative (n) ⊙	distance learning (n phr)	principle (adj)
aspect (n) ⊙	employability (n)	pursue (v) ⊙
assignment (n) ⊙	establishment (n) ⊙	regard (v) ⊙
campus (n) ⊙	examination (n) ⊙	semester (n)
community (n) ⊙	in-depth (adj)	seminar (n) ⊙
concrete (adj)	illiteracy (n)	significant (adj)
core (adj)	journal (n) ⊙	specific (adj)
core principles (n phr)	lecturer (n) ⊙	stigma (n) ⊙
credible alternative (n phr)	modern phenomenon (n phr)	technological advances (n phr)
deadline (n)	motivation (n) ⊙	term (n) ⊙
degree (n) ⊙	online degree (n phr)	tutor (n) ⊙
discipline (n) ⊙	peer (n) ⊙	virtual (adj)
dissertation (n) ⊙	plagiarism (n)	virtual classroom (n phr)

⊙ = high-frequency words in the Cambridge Academic Corpus

MEDICINE

LEARNING OBJECTIVES

Watch and listen
Watch and understand a video about doctors using virtual reality to help patients.

Reading skill
Annotate a text.

Critical thinking
Evaluate ideas.

Grammar
Use articles; use transitions to show concession.

Academic writing skill
Use sentence variety.

Writing task
Write an opinion essay.

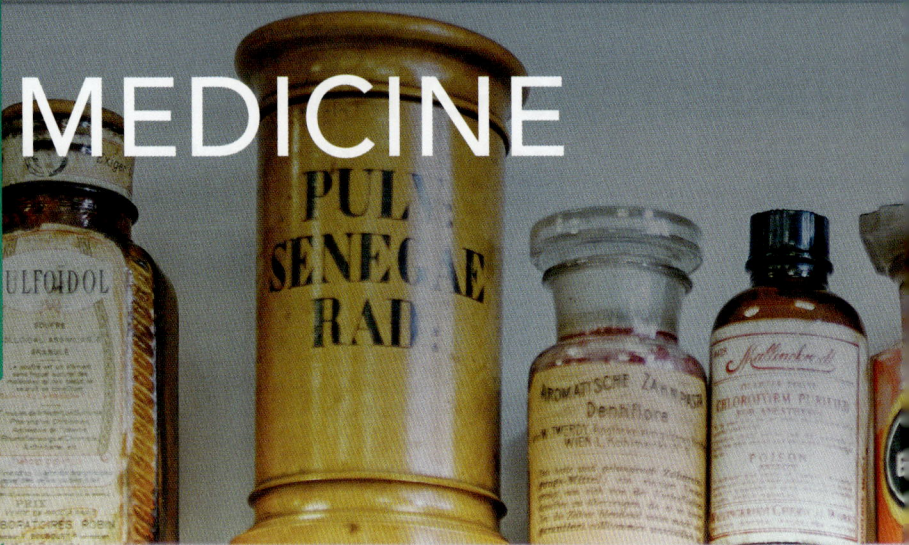

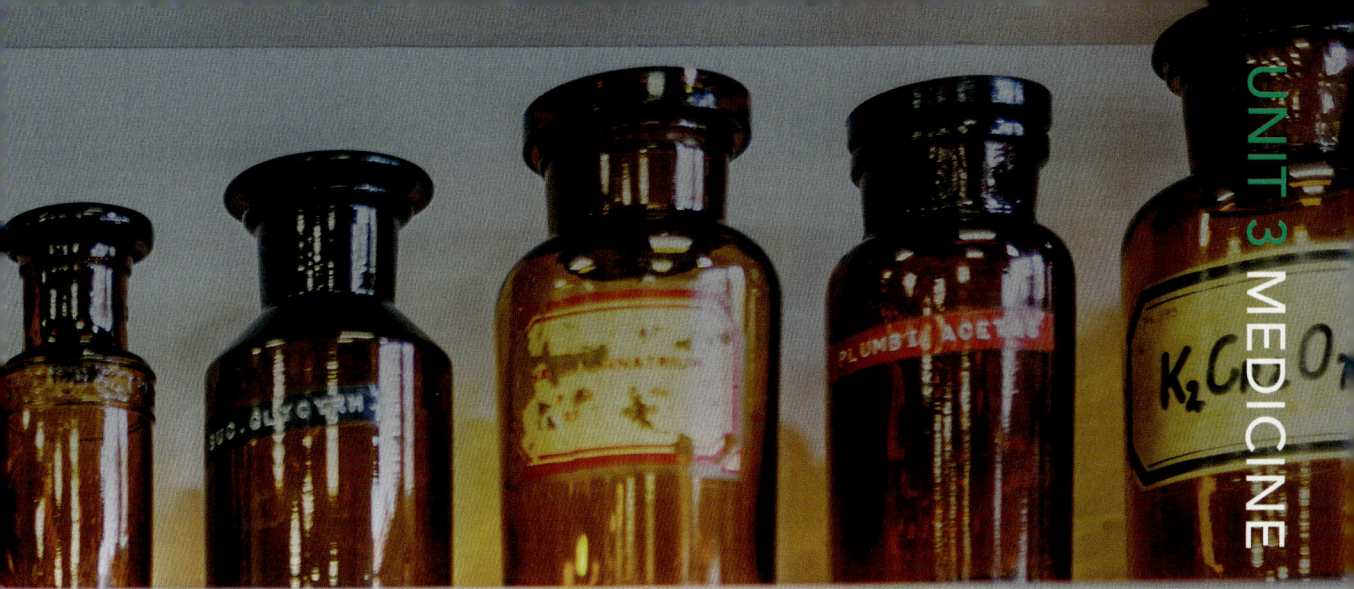

UNLOCK YOUR KNOWLEDGE

Work with a partner. Discuss the questions.

1 Which of the following types of alternative medicine have you heard of? What do you know about them?
- acupuncture
- homeopathy
- hypnotherapy
- reiki

2 Have you used alternative medicine? If not, would you consider doing so? Why / Why not?

3 Why do you think some people prefer to use alternative medicines?

4 Do you know of any popular natural remedies for illness in your country, for example a cold or a sore throat?

WATCH AND LISTEN

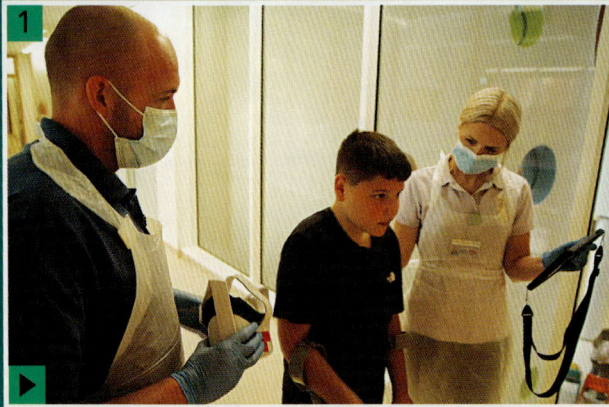

PREPARING TO WATCH

ACTIVATING YOUR KNOWLEDGE

1 Work with a partner and answer the questions.

1 What is virtual reality? Have you ever used it? If so, how was it?
2 In what ways could virtual reality be used in medicine?

PREDICTING CONTENT USING VISUALS

2 Look at the photos from the video. Discuss the questions with a partner.

1 What do all the photos have in common?
2 How do you think each type of technology is being used?
3 Why do you think this technology is being used as opposed to more traditional methods?

| GLOSSARY

state of mind (n) how you are feeling at a particular time

physiotherapy (n) the treatment of problems of the muscles, joints, or nerves

rehabilitation (n) to help someone live a normal life again after they have had a serious illness

mobility (n) the ability to move freely or be easily moved

tumour (n) a mass of diseased cells that might become a lump or cause illness

WHILE WATCHING

UNDERSTANDING MAIN IDEAS

3 ▶ Watch the video. Write *T* (true) or *F* (false) or *DNS* (does not say) next to the statements below. Correct the false statements.

_____ 1 VR guides patients on how to exercise properly.
_____ 2 VR can make physiotherapy sessions more enjoyable.
_____ 3 Patients often work harder because they are distracted by VR.
_____ 4 Doctors use VR to investigate tumours because it is easier to understand their size.

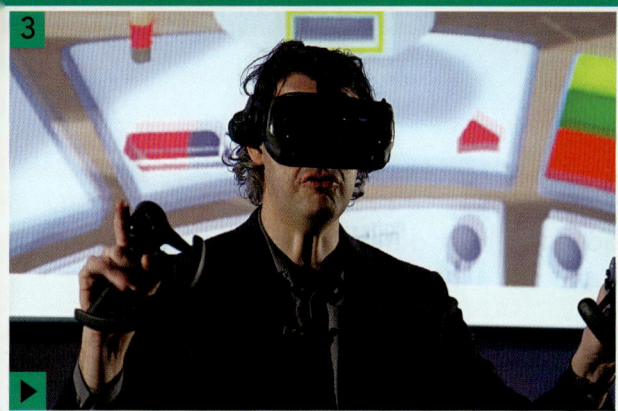

4 ▶ Watch again and complete the sentences using words from the video. Use no more than THREE WORDS.

1 Doctors hope a unique combination of in-bed cycling and virtual reality will change weak patients' _____ .

2 12-year-old Noel has a _____ which means frequent surgery and physiotherapy to help him walk.

3 Chiropractor Matt Flanagan was one of the first to use this method in the UK. He uses scans of his patients' _____ to create a virtual tour for him.

4 The team have shown that understanding the _____ in a tumour can help predict how a patient's condition might progress and respond to treatment.

5 Work with a partner and discuss the questions. Give reasons for your answers.

1 For the patient Noel, what are the physical and mental benefits of using VR?

2 Why do you think Matt Flanigan uses a scan of a patient's spine to create a virtual tour for them?

DISCUSSION

6 Work with a partner and answer the questions.

1 Do you think that using VR with patients will appeal equally to all age groups? Why / Why not?

2 What might be some of the potential drawbacks of using VR within healthcare?

UNDERSTANDING DETAIL

MAKING INFERENCES

READING 1

PREPARING TO READ

1 Read the sentences and choose the best definition for the words in bold.

1 After my knee **surgery**, my leg was sore for several weeks.
   a taking medicine for a period of time after you are sick
   b the cutting open of the body to repair a damaged part

2 Two **symptoms** of the common cold are coughing and sneezing.
   a types of illnesses
   b reactions or feelings of illness which are caused by a disease

3 Doctors are usually big **proponents** of regular exercise for their patients as exercise can have many positive effects on health.
   a people who support a particular idea or plan of action
   b people who argue against an idea

4 The new treatment is **controversial**. Some people think it has not been tested enough, while others believe in it.
   a causing disagreement or discussion
   b causing agreement

5 The government has **funded** the hospital in my neighbourhood by donating £5 million of last year's tax money.
   a given land for a new building
   b provided money to pay for something

6 It is dangerous to consume illegal **substances** because they have not been approved by the country's medical authorities.
   a foods which are unhealthy
   b materials with particular physical characteristics

7 My grandmother is afraid to use **conventional** treatment for her illness. Instead, she drinks a tea made from a variety of plants.
   a following the usual practices
   b alternative and non-traditional

8 Heart disease is the **chief** cause of death for people in the United States. It kills more people than any other disease.
   a most important or main
   b most uncommon

2 You are going to read an article about the homeopathy debate. Look quickly at the article. Look at the title, subheads and introduction. Decide which statement best describes what the article is about.

1 The article presents the arguments for and against conventional types of medicine.
2 The article discusses why some alternative medical treatments are free.
3 The article gives two people's opinions on the effectiveness of using homeopathy.
4 The article discusses a range of alternative medical treatments.

WHILE READING

Annotating a text

Annotating a text while you read can help you remember information a lot better. When you annotate, you mark up the text and add notes in the margin as you read. When you read about different writers' opinions on a single subject, it is a good idea to highlight each writer's opinions in a different colour, then underline the support each writer gives for their opinions. You can also react to a writer's opinions by writing notes in the margin, putting a star next to the strongest reasons and support, etc.

SKILLS

3 Read the article on the homeopathy debate. Highlight each writer's opinion in a different colour and underline the support each writer provides. Write notes in the margin as you read.

4 Read the article again. Write *T* (true), *F* (false) or *DNS* (does not say) next to the statements. Correct the false statements.

_____ 1 The majority of countries use alternative rather than conventional medicine.
_____ 2 Supporters of homeopathy believe that patients should have choices in their treatment.
_____ 3 More than two-thirds of doctors in the UK are against state-funded homeopathic treatment.
_____ 4 Traditional Indian doctors frequently use homeopathy.
_____ 5 Abigail Hayes thinks that homeopathic remedies only work because of the placebo effect.
_____ 6 In the UK, people currently have a choice as to what treatment they can get.
_____ 7 Homeopathic healthcare is not available in the United States.
_____ 8 Weak, highly diluted liquids are a common form of homeopathic treatment.

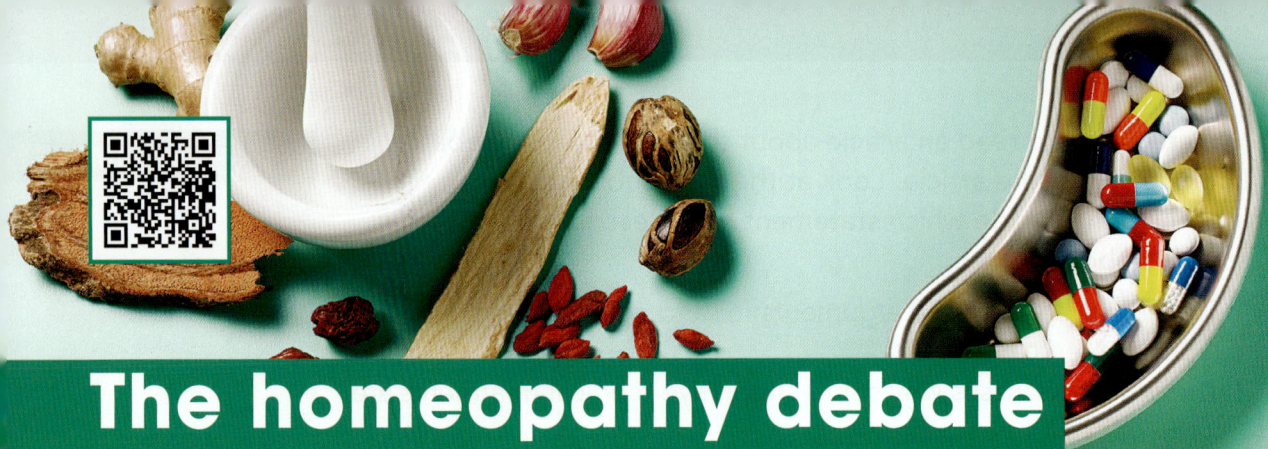

The homeopathy debate

1 Most national health systems use **conventional** medicine, meaning that illnesses are treated using drugs and **surgery**. However, there is also a range of alternative medical treatments to choose from. One **controversial** treatment is homeopathy. Homeopathic remedies are highly diluted[1] mixtures of natural **substances**, such as plants and minerals, which may cause the **symptoms** of a disease in healthy people. The idea is that they will cure similar symptoms in sick people. Supporters of homeopathy believe that it can be effective. Others argue, however, that homeopathy does not work and agree that the state should not **fund** it. Here, one **proponent** and one critic present their cases.

Homeopathy should be state funded
by Abigail Hayes (Professional Homeopath)

2 The British National Health Service was founded to provide free healthcare to people who needed it. Since it was founded in 1948, patients have been able to get homeopathic treatment, and there's no good reason why this shouldn't continue. Most importantly, it's estimated that homeopathic treatments only cost the NHS around 4 million pounds a year. This is a fraction of the cost paid out to conventional drug companies. Many doctors regularly recommend homeopathic treatments, since they are cheap and popular. Therefore, I find it difficult to understand why the government is considering cutting funding for them. Why shouldn't people be allowed to make their own health choices? They have this freedom in other aspects of their lives – for example, which school to send their children to – so why not in terms of their healthcare?

Homeopathic treatments: not too expensive, allow patient choice, effective, use 'power of belief'

3 As for the critics who argue that homeopathy doesn't work, I could give hundreds of examples of patients who have been cured by my treatment. On top of that, there's plenty of research which shows the benefits it can bring. Homeopathy wouldn't have survived so long if it were complete nonsense. It has much more than just a placebo effect[2]. Too much emphasis is sometimes put on providing 'proof' of why something works. Belief is just as powerful.

Homeopathy should not be state funded
by Dr Piers Wehner (NHS General Practitioner)

4 We don't really know whether homeopathy helps people feel better because of the remedies themselves or because people believe they will work. Some people just feel better when they get personal care and attention from their homeopathic practitioner. For me and many others in my profession, there is absolutely no proof that says homeopathic treatment works. The government's **chief** scientist confirmed this when he said there was 'no real evidence' to support homeopathy. We live in difficult economic times, and every penny the government spends should be checked to ensure that it is not wasted. In fact, 75% of British doctors are against the state funding of homeopathy.

5 One of the main arguments put forward by supporters of homeopathy is that this therapy doesn't cause any damage. However, people may think they are treating their illness by taking homeopathic remedies when there is actually no scientific evidence that this is true. Even more seriously, patients who rely on homeopathy alone for treating life-threatening illnesses like cancer could be taking a big risk. The cancer might no longer be treatable by proven methods if the patient has waited too long trying homeopathy. This can cost lives.

[1]**diluted** (adj) made weaker by mixing with something else, such as water
[2]**placebo effect** (n) an improvement in a patient's condition caused only by his or her belief in the benefit of the treatment

IDENTIFYING OPINIONS

5 Which of the two people in the article would agree with the statements?

	Abigail Hayes	Piers Wehner
1 The doctor says it's too late to help her now. If only she'd gone to see him earlier.		
2 Look, if I don't want to risk the side effects of conventional drugs, why should I have to?		
3 When I see proper clinical trials which prove the effectiveness of homeopathy, then I'll change my mind.		
4 The mind has incredibly strong healing powers.		
5 If it means we could stop paying all that money for drugs, then I'm for it.		
6 It worked. I don't know why. It doesn't seem possible, but I'm just happy that it worked.		
7 This is serious. You can keep taking the homeopathic treatment as well, if you want, but you've got to see a doctor.		
8 If three-quarters of professionals are against it, I'm against it.		

READING BETWEEN THE LINES

6 Work with a partner. Discuss possible reasons for the statements. Then say whether you agree with them or not.

MAKING INFERENCES

1 Homeopathic treatment is much cheaper than conventional medicine.
2 Belief is as powerful as medicine.
3 Personal care and attention make people feel better.
4 There is no real proof that homeopathy works.
5 Doctors need to see scientific evidence.

DISCUSSION

7 Work with a partner. Discuss the questions.

1 Do you think the placebo effect works? Why / Why not?
2 Do you think the government should fund alternative medicines, such as homeopathy? Why / Why not?
3 What do you think the benefits of homeopathic medicines are over traditional medicines?

READING 2

PREPARING TO READ

UNDERSTANDING
KEY VOCABULARY

1 You are going to read an article about healthcare systems. In pairs discuss the words in the box. Use a dictionary to help you.

> **burden** (n) **consultation** (n) **contribution** (n) **labour** (n)
> **regardless** (adv) **safety net** (n phr) **treatment** (n)

2 Complete the paragraph using the words from Exercise 1.

Paying for private healthcare can be a huge financial a) _____ for many people. Attending a b) _____ to get advice on a medical issue or receiving c) _____ for an illness can cost a fortune. Therefore, many people choose to take out private medical insurance and this d) _____, which is often paid annually, can provide a good e) _____ against any unforeseen medical issues. Nevertheless, good medical care should be provided for all people, f) _____ of wealth. Whether you work in manual g) _____ or have an office job, everyone should receive the same level of healthcare.

USING YOUR
KNOWLEDGE

3 Work with a partner. Answer the questions.

1 Do you have to pay for healthcare in your country? What healthcare provision, if any, does your government pay for?
2 What do you know about healthcare systems in other countries?
3 Read the descriptions of the healthcare systems a–d below. Match them to a country from the box.

> Democratic Republic of Congo   Germany   UAE   UK

a This country spends more on healthcare per person than almost all of its neighbouring countries. Healthcare is free (or almost free) for everyone. This is paid for by the government.
b Most workers have to pay for government health insurance from their salaries or buy insurance on their own.
c Healthcare is expensive and more than 10% of the population do not have health coverage. Those who are not enrolled in government schemes have to pay for health insurance.
d Under the National Health Service, all workers pay National Insurance according to how much they earn. This is collected by the government and used to pay for hospitals and other medical treatment.

4 Skim the article. Read the title, introduction and topic sentences. Decide which statement best describes what the article is about.

1 The article criticizes government policies.
2 The article focuses on private funding as it relates to healthcare.
3 The article examines different kinds of healthcare.
4 The article discusses the role of medication in healthcare.

SHOULD HEALTHCARE BE FREE?

1 Who pays for healthcare? The answer varies from country to country. While in some nations it is completely free for all residents, in others people often receive their health insurance through their employer. There are also places where you can only see a doctor if you pay. Often, a patient is faced with the choice of medium-quality but cheap care versus high-quality but expensive care. Unfortunately, providing healthcare to an entire nation of citizens is a complicated matter. While different healthcare systems have various advantages and disadvantages, no system is ideal.

Free public healthcare

2 Within the countries which provide free public healthcare, there are many models. In some countries, **consultations**, **treatment** and medicines are free to all citizens. This may be paid for directly by the government, perhaps funded by the country's valuable natural resources that the government owns. Other countries collect money from citizens through taxes based on their income. Workers pay according to how much they earn, and employers also make a **contribution**. Hospitals and other medical services are then provided and run by the government. There may also be some private medical services which people can choose to buy. The advantage of systems such as these is clear: free basic healthcare for all, **regardless** of income. However, it is a very expensive system and, as life expectancy and costs rise, many countries are facing either an unsustainable financial **burden**, or a drop in the quality of services and facilities provided.

Private healthcare

3 In countries where citizens use private providers, healthcare is only available to patients who pay for it, and healthcare providers are commercial companies. In wealthier countries, most citizens take out health insurance to cover their potential medical costs. However, not everyone can afford this, and some governments have a scheme which gives financial assistance to those who need urgent medical care but are unable to afford it. In other nations, there is no such **safety net**, and those who cannot pay simply do not get the healthcare they need, unless they can get financial help. The disadvantages of this system are obvious: not only are individuals deprived of the medical attention they need, but also the lack of preventative medicine means that infectious diseases can quickly spread. One advantage, however, is that commercial organizations can sometimes provide higher-quality care than struggling government-funded ones.

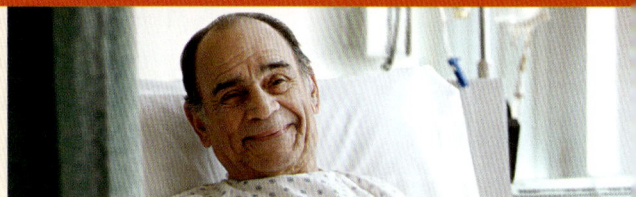

A mixed system

4 In many countries, there is a mix of public and private funding. This system requires all its citizens to take out health insurance. This is deducted from salaries by the employer, who also has to make a contribution for each worker. Citizens are able to choose their healthcare providers, which may be public or private. However, in some systems, private companies are not permitted to make a profit from providing basic healthcare. This model provides more flexibility than either the public or private models, and ensures access to healthcare for all. However, it has been criticized for driving up the cost of **labour**, which can lead to unemployment.

Conclusion

5 Most of us will likely agree that no healthcare system is perfect. Several countries are now considering a combination of the models for their national health systems. The challenge is to find a system which provides a high-quality level of healthcare to all citizens, but which is also affordable and practical. Whether or not such a system can work remains to be seen.

WHILE READING

5 Underline the key features of each healthcare system mentioned in the article (an example has been done for you). Write notes about each healthcare system mentioned.

6 Read the article again. Write *T* (true) or *F* (false) next to the statements. Correct the false statements, and underline the part of the article where you found your answer.

_____ **1** In a mixed system it is only the employer who has to contribute towards healthcare.

_____ **2** The writer believes that some countries have achieved the perfect solution to providing good healthcare for all.

_____ **3** In free healthcare systems funded by taxes all employees contribute the same amount of money.

_____ **4** In some mixed systems private medical companies are forbidden from being commercial.

_____ **5** In some countries which do not provide free medical care, not everyone has access to help, even in an emergency.

7 Reading comprehension questions often do not use the same words as the text. Match the words from the text (1–8) to the correct synonyms (a–h).

Match the following words from the text to their synonym.

1 access	a perfect
2 make profit	b given
3 ideal	c people
4 funded	d forbidden
5 citizens	e commercial
6 provided	f emergency
7 not permitted	g get
8 urgent	h paid for

READING BETWEEN THE LINES

8 Work with a partner. Answer the questions based on the information in the article.

1 Which healthcare system might a person with a long-term illness prefer? Why?

2 Which system might a person with a high income prefer? Why?

DISCUSSION

9 Work with a partner. Use ideas from Reading 1 and Reading 2 to discuss the following questions.

1 Which healthcare system (public, private or mixed) do you think is the best? Why?
2 Have you had any experience of your own country's healthcare system? Was it a good experience? Why / Why not?

WRITING

10 What do you value about your country's healthcare system and what do you think could be improved? Write 100–150 words.

⊙ LANGUAGE DEVELOPMENT

MEDICAL VOCABULARY

1 In pairs discuss the meaning of each of these words and then attach them to one of the categories below. Use a dictionary to help you.

> diabetes   drugs   obesity   pharmaceutical   prescriptions
> preventable   surgeon   ward

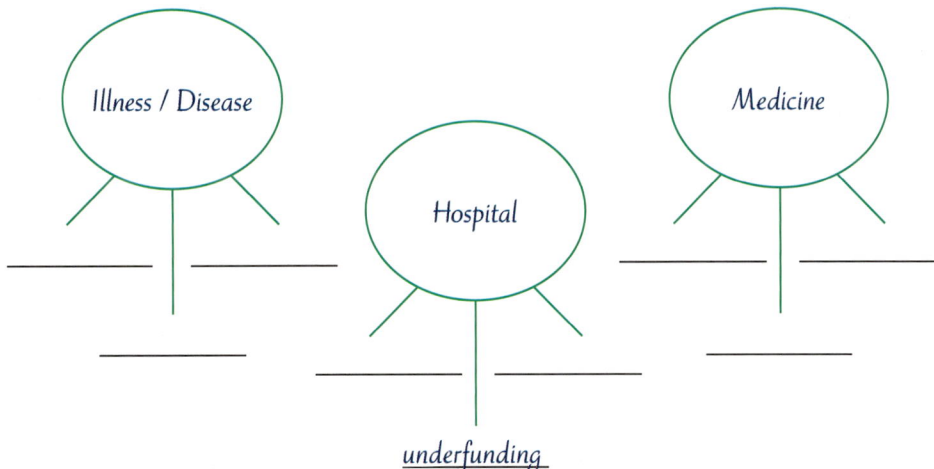

Illness / Disease

Hospital

Medicine

underfunding

2 Complete the following questions with a word from Exercise 1. Then discuss with a partner.

1 Do you think some illnesses are _____ ?
2 Should _____ be free for everyone?
3 What is the best way to tackle the growing issue of _____ ?

ACADEMIC VOCABULARY

1 Read the questions below and try to understand the meaning of the words in bold through their context (the words around them).

- A surgeon has to be very **precise** when performing an operation. Is this type of work best completed by a robot?
- Do you think doctors should only subscribe to **conventional** methods of treatment?
- Do you think that providing healthcare for a country is a very **complex** issue, or can it be easily resolved?
- Do you think there is **adequate** healthcare provision for the elderly in your country?
- Do you think it should be **illegal** for pharmaceutical companies to make large profits on their medicines?
- Have you always found the doctors and nurses you have met to be **professional** in their approach?
- Do you think you do enough **physical** exercise to maintain a healthy lifestyle?
- Have you ever experienced any **adverse** effects after having any medicines or vaccines?

2 Complete the table below with one of the words in bold:

Definition	Adjective
1 having a negative or harmful effect on something	
2 having the qualities that you connect with trained and skilled people	
3 against the law	
4 connected with the body	
5 difficult to understand or find an answer to because of having many different parts	
6 enough or satisfactory for a particular purpose	
7 traditional and ordinary	
8 exact and accurate	

3 In pairs see if you can produce the noun from each of these adjectives and then create a sentence. Use a dictionary if needed.

*I really appreciated the nurse's **professionalism** when she gave me the injection.*

4 In pairs or small groups discuss the questions in Exercise 1.

WRITING

CRITICAL THINKING

At the end of this unit, you will write an opinion essay. Look at this unit's writing task below.

> Some people believe that disease prevention is the responsibility of the individual, while others believe it is the role of the government. Discuss both views and give your opinion. Write 350–400 words.

1 Brainstorm different ways in which diseases can be prevented. Write a separate point next to each number.

REMEMBER

1	6
2	7
3	8
4	9
5	10

2 Compare your answers with a partner. Add any useful points to your own list.

3 Look at the Likert scale below. Think about whose responsibility it is to prevent diseases that affect people in your society: the government, individuals, or somewhere in between. Circle the number which corresponds to your view.

EVALUATE

4 Compare your answers with a partner. Do you agree or disagree? Discuss and make any changes you feel are necessary.

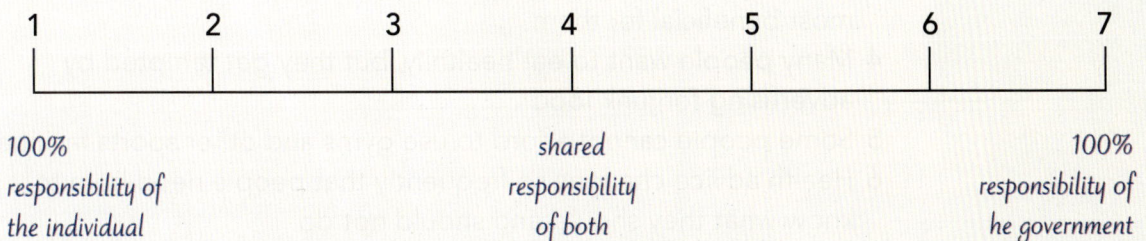

1   2   3   4   5   6   7

100%
responsibility of
the individual

shared
responsibility
of both

100%
responsibility of
he government

5 Look at the work you did in Exercises 1 and 3 on page 71 and answer these questions.

1 Do you think that the government or individuals should be more responsible for preventing diseases?
2 Will the items you have listed be practical or easy to achieve for the individuals? for the government?

6 Work in groups. Look at the list of actions that people can take to avoid becoming sick. Try to agree on the five most important actions.

> avoiding sunburn   brushing your teeth
> doing what makes you happy   drinking enough water
> eating healthy food   getting enough fresh air
> getting recommended vaccinations   getting regular exercise
> not smoking   reducing stress   sleeping enough
> washing your hands frequently

7 Look at your list of the five most important actions and answer the questions.

1 How can individuals and families help themselves to take these actions?
2 How can the government help people to take these actions?

8 Read the statements. Which statements are in favour of individual responsibility for preventative healthcare? Which are against?

1 Healthcare is extremely expensive for governments, and medical evidence strongly suggests that lifestyle is a major indicator of health.
2 People should be able to choose their own lifestyle.
3 People have different situations, so they need to decide what is most beneficial for them.
4 Many people want to eat healthily, but they get tempted by advertising for junk food.
5 Some people cannot afford to use gyms and other sports facilities.
6 Health advice changes so frequently that people need help to know what they should and should not do.
7 The easiest thing is to do nothing, which means many people do not take the steps needed to improve their health.
8 Health education is needed, and not only in schools.
9 If people do not take personal responsibility, they will lose the ability to make good choices.

GRAMMAR FOR WRITING

ARTICLES

Articles are some of the most common words in the English language. Knowing how to use them properly is therefore important to the accuracy of academic writing. The three types of articles are outlined below:

Definite article (*the*)

a) *The* is used to refer to something specific which has been mentioned before:

Malaria is a disease which affects certain countries. **The disease** *is spread by mosquitoes.*

b) *The* is used for nouns when there is only one example of something:

The US healthcare policy *changed in 2014.*

c) *The* is used for ordinal numbers:

This is **the second operation** *that she has had.*

d) *The* is used with superlative adjectives:

Heart disease is **the most common** *health problem in our society.*

e) *The* is used before certain countries

The United Kingdom *has a National Health System.*

Indefinite article (*a/an*)

a) The indefinite articles *a* and *an* are used to introduce single, countable nouns which are not specified:

A doctor *spoke to her patient about* **an important health risk.**

b) If the noun starts with a consonant, we use *a*. If the noun starts with a vowel sound, we use *an*:

A good healthcare system *is* **an important factor** *for citizens' health.*

c) If the noun starts with a vowel but has a consonant sound, we use *a*:

She works at **a university hospital.**

Zero article (Ø)

a) No articles are needed for uncountable nouns when talking about things in general:

Water and **oxygen** *are vital for* **life.**

b) No articles are needed for plural countable nouns when talking about things or people in general:

Nurses *generally work hard.*

c) No articles are needed for some proper nouns such as the names of most countries or people:

Doctor Ahmadi *is from* **Jordan.**

The use of articles in a discursive essay

When you **begin an academic essay or paragraph**, it is **common** to start with a **generalization**.

Example:

A healthy diet is the key to long life.
Good health is important for everyone.

Use *a/an* for singular nouns and zero article for uncountable and plural nouns.

If you refer to a specific noun that is familiar to your reader, use ***the***:

People with that disease know that **the drugs** are cheaper abroad than they are here. (The reader understands which drugs are referred to by the context.)

1 Use the rules from pages 73–74 to complete the paragraph below with *a*, *an*, *the* or zero article (Ø).

Reflexology is [1]_____ complimentary therapy, and it involves applying gentle pressure to your feet or sometimes hands. [2]_____ idea behind the therapy is that there are certain points on our feet and hands which correspond to [3]_____ organs and glands on our body. Therefore, by massaging and pressing these points, energy pathways in [4]_____ body can be stimulated. If these energy pathways are blocked, then [5]_____ aim of [6]_____ reflexology is to unblock them. Reflexology can also be [7]_____ very relaxing experience and helps many people with feelings of stress and anxiety.

2 Discuss the following questions with a partner. Think about your use of articles when you answer the questions.

1 Have you ever tried reflexology? If yes, was it a good experience?
2 If you haven't tried reflexology, would you? Why / Why not?

TRANSITIONS TO SHOW CONCESSION (THE OPPOSITE OPINION)

When you present an argument in writing, you often need to mention opposing arguments. You can introduce opposing views by using certain phrases which show that there is a difference of opinion.

Homeopathy seems to be ineffective. **Other people claim that** *it works.*

Simple language of concession followed by a clause or a sentence:

Homeopathy seems to be ineffective, **but** *some people claim that it works.*

Homeopathy seems to be ineffective. **However**, *some people claim that it works.*

More complex language of concession

Followed by a clause:

Homeopathy seems to be ineffective. **Nevertheless**, *people still use it.*

Even though / Despite the fact that / In spite of the fact that *homeopathy seems to be ineffective, people still use it.*

Followed by a noun phrase:

Despite / In spite of *its ineffectiveness, people still use it.*

3 Complete each sentence using one of the concession words or phrases.

1 People who need expensive medicines are often willing to pay a lot of money for them, _____ the cost.

2 _____ the results are not scientifically proven, my mother uses this homeopathic remedy.

3 Some people say that alternative therapies do not work. _____ they are very effective.

4 Government-provided healthcare is free for citizens. _____ , they do have to pay taxes to support it.

5 _____ the fact he struggled to walk; he still made the effort to try every day.

ACADEMIC WRITING SKILLS

SENTENCE VARIETY

SKILLS

Your academic writing will be stronger if you can **vary the types of sentences that you write**. You can combine longer, more complex sentences with shorter, more straightforward ones to create a text which is more interesting and has a stronger overall flow.

You can create more interesting sentences by:
- varying the length of sentences in a text
- beginning sentences with subordinate clauses
- using conjunctions to make compound sentences
- beginning sentences with prepositions
- using relative clauses to combine information.

For example, you can begin a sentence with a subordinate clause such as 'Although it is expensive, …', or with a prepositional phrase such as 'In some countries, … '. Notice the difference between these two texts:

A *Many people do not have access to healthcare. This may be because their country's government does not provide it. It could also be because they cannot afford it. This is a problem.*

All of the sentences start with a subject (e.g. 'Many people'), then have a verb (e.g. 'have'). Compare this sentence:

B *Because their government does not provide it, <u>or because it is too expensive</u>, many people do not have healthcare. This is a problem.*

Text B comes across as better writing and has a better flow. The sentences do not all follow the 'subject + verb' structure, and the first sentence here begins with a subordinate clause. Now look at these two texts.

C *The healthcare system in my country is not ideal. It works adequately for the rich and the poor. It does not work adequately for middle-class citizens. This is unacceptable.*

D *<u>In my country</u>, the healthcare system, <u>which works adequately for the rich and the poor</u>, does not work well for middle-class citizens. <u>This is unacceptable</u>.*

Text D uses sentence variety: starting the sentence with a preposition, and using relative clauses to combine information.

1 Follow the instructions to write sentences with the words provided.

   1 Write two sentences: a longer one, and then a shorter one.
People / should / not / take / medicine / prescribed / someone / else / is / dangerous
People should not take medicine that is prescribed for someone else. This is dangerous.

   2 Write a sentence that begins with a subordinate clause.
Even though / illness / heavily / researched / cure / not / found

   3 Write a sentence that contains a relative clause.
This / hospital / I / was / born

   4 Write two sentences: a longer one, and then a shorter one.
All / people / our / society / access / affordable / healthcare / their / right

   5 Write a sentence that begins with a preposition.
He / studied / medicine / university

   6 Write a sentence which uses a conjunction.
Healthy lifestyle / can / prevent / disease / help / you / live longer

WRITING TASK

Some people believe that disease prevention is the responsibility of the individual, while others believe it is the role of the government. Discuss both views and give your opinion. Write 350/400 words.

PLAN

1 Work with a partner. Using your ideas from Critical thinking on page 1, discuss how you could complete the essay outline below.

	Your notes
Paragraph 1: Introduce the topic / your opinion / thesis statement (about 50–100 words)	
Paragraph 2: Why is it the responsibility of the individual? (about 100 words)	
Paragraph 3: Why is it the responsibility of the government? (about 100 words)	
Paragraph 4: summary & re-instate your own opinion (about 50–100 words)	

2 Use your ideas from Exercise 1 and create an essay outline for your essay.

3 Refer to the Task checklist on page 78 as you prepare your essay.

WRITE A FIRST DRAFT

4 Write your essay using the outline.

REVISE

5 Use the Task checklist to review your essay for content and structure.

TASK CHECKLIST	✔
Did you give your opinion in your writing and make it clear what your response to the question is in the introduction?	
Did you use sentence variety?	
Did you mention opposing ideas?	
Did you check the word count?	

6 Make any necessary changes to your essay.

EDIT

7 Use the Language checklist to edit your essay for language errors.

LANGUAGE CHECKLIST	✔
Did you use articles (the, a/an, zero article) correctly?	
Did you use transitions for concession (despite, although, however, etc.) to show opposing views to your own arguments?	
Did you use an appropriate range of medical and academic vocabulary?	
Did you use the adjective forms of academic nouns?	

8 Make any necessary changes to your essay.

OBJECTIVES REVIEW

1 Check your learning objectives for this unit. Write *3, 2* or *1* for each objective.

3 = very well   2 = well   1 = not so well

I can …

watch and understand a video about doctors using VR to help patients. _____

annotate a text. _____

evaluate ideas. _____

use articles. _____

use transitions to show concession. _____

use sentence variety. _____

write an opinion essay. _____

2 Use the *Unlock* Digital Workbook for more practice with this unit's learning objectives.

UNL◯CK
**DIGITAL
WORKBOOK**

WORDLIST

adequate (adj)	illegal (adj)	professional (adj)
adverse (adj)	labour (n) ⊙	proponent (n) ⊙
burden (n) ⊙	medical (adj)	regardless (adv)
chief (adj)	mobility (n) ⊙	safety net (n phr)
complex (adj)	obesity (n) ⊙	substances (n)
consultation (n) ⊙	patent (n) ⊙	surgeon (n) ⊙
contribution (n) ⊙	pharmaceutical (n)	surgery (n) ⊙
controversial (adj)	physical (adj)	symptoms (n)
conventional (adj)	physiotherapy (n)	treatment (n) ⊙
diabetes (n) ⊙	precise (adj)	tumour (n) ⊙
drug (n) ⊙	prescription (n) ⊙	underfunding (n)
epidemic (n) ⊙	preventable illness (n phr)	ward (n) ⊙
fund (v) ⊙		

⊙ = high-frequency words in the Cambridge Academic Corpus

THE ENVIRONMENT

LEARNING OBJECTIVES

Watch and listen
Watch and understand a video about population and water.

Reading skill
Identify cohesive devices.

Critical thinking
Analyze a case study; evaluate arguments.

Grammar
Express solutions using *it*.

Academic writing skill
Develop ideas; use parallel structure.

Writing task
Write a problem-solution essay.

UNLOCK YOUR KNOWLEDGE

Work with a partner. Discuss the questions.

1 Can you think of any natural disasters which have happened recently either locally or around the world? What impact did it have on the local community?

2 Why do you think natural disasters are becoming increasingly common?

3 In what ways can society help protect the environment? What do you do to be environmentally friendly?

WATCH AND LISTEN

PREPARING TO WATCH

ACTIVATING YOUR KNOWLEDGE

1 Tick (✔) the statements that you agree with. Compare your answers with a partner.

1 ☐ There is an unlimited amount of clean drinking water.
2 ☐ We are losing precious natural resources.
3 ☐ Scientists are developing new ways to clean water.
4 ☐ As the population grows, there's less access to clean water.

PREDICTING CONTENT USING VISUALS

2 Look at the pictures from the video. Discuss the questions with your partner.

1 What parts of the world are experiencing a water shortage?
2 What factors lead to water shortages?

┃ GLOSSARY

polar ice cap (n) a thick layer of ice near the North or South Pole which permanently covers an area of land

distribution (n) the way something is divided and shared in a group or area

transform (v) to change something completely, often to improve it

reservoir (n) a natural or artificial lake for storing and supplying water

WHILE WATCHING

UNDERSTANDING MAIN IDEAS

3 ▶ Watch the video. Write *T* (true), *F* (false) or *DNS* (does not say) next to the statements. Correct the false statements.

_____ 1 Only 2.5% of the Earth's water is available for human use.
_____ 2 Transforming deserts, producing energy from rivers and building cities needs over half of our available fresh water.
_____ 3 Access to clean drinking water is a critical problem for more than a billion people.
_____ 4 Water shortages are the result of people living in deserts.

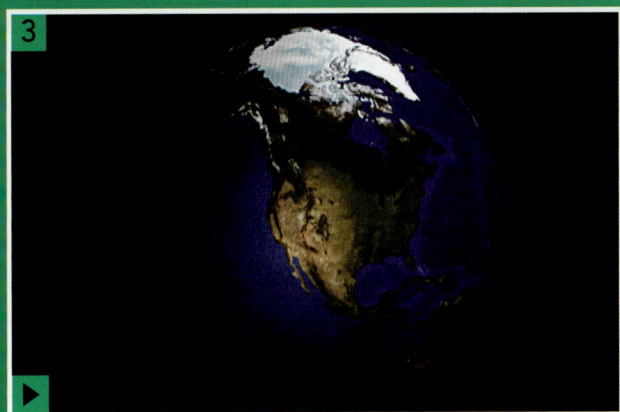

4 ▶ Watch again. Complete the summary.

Water covers about [1]_____ of the Earth's surface. However, only a small fraction of this water is suitable for human use. While there is no more water on the planet than there was in the distant past, the [2]_____ of water has changed. This is partly due to an increase in [3]_____; as the number of people on the planet grows, so does the water crisis. Several factors contribute to the shortage: poor [4]_____ , politics, poverty and simply living in a dry part of the world. Cities like Mexico City are especially at risk. Shops which sell water are becoming increasingly [5]_____ . Changes in the Earth's water distribution can be seen from [6]_____ . Places like the Aral Sea and Lake Chad in the Sahara Desert have visibly changed due to [7]_____ and overuse.

5 Work with a partner. Discuss the questions. Give reasons to support your answers.

1 Why do you think only a small fraction of the Earth's water is available for human use?
2 What can be done to preserve and protect fresh water?
3 How does education help in conserving water?

DISCUSSION

6 Discuss the questions with your partner.

1 Have you ever observed any changes in water access in your city or country? Describe the change.
2 How often do you purchase bottles of water? How common are bottles of water today? Do they present any environmental or economic concerns?

READING

READING 1

PREPARING TO READ

1 Read the two paragraphs and write the correct form of each bold word next to the correct definition.

A Scientists have not yet **identified** which kind of storm is approaching the Caribbean. The last storm was a hurricane which had a **devastating** effect on the buildings near the beach, as many of them were destroyed. To prepare for this storm, there are several important **measures** which people in that area should take. For example, it is **crucial** to have plenty of water, some torches and batteries.

1 _____ (n) a method for dealing with a situation
2 _____ (v) to recognize something and say what that thing is
3 _____ (adj) extremely important or necessary
4 _____ (adj) causing a lot of damage or destruction

B Our **community** is located by the ocean and contains about 75 families. We are all working towards a **reduction** in the damage done by storms here. Part of that includes sharing the **maintenance** costs of planting sea grass and building sand fences. In the past, some families were **criticized** for not contributing their fair share of these maintenance costs.

5 _____ (n) the people living in one particular area
6 _____ (n) the work needed to keep something in good condition
7 _____ (n) the act of making something smaller in size or amount
8 _____ (v) to express disapproval of someone or something

2 Look at the photos of different natural disasters and ways to prevent damage from natural disasters. Label the photos with the words from the box.

| dam | flood barrier | levee | hurricane | sandbagging | tsunami |

1 _____

2 _____

3 _____

4 _____

5 _____

6 _____

3 Skim the interview with a disaster-mitigation expert. Which title below is best for the interview? Why?

1 Controlling the flow
2 What to do about risk
3 A way to protect people from flooding
4 Protect your house against flooding

Disaster mitigation

1 The world has always had to face water-based natural disasters such as tsunamis and hurricanes. In an illuminating[1] interview, *Water Management Monthly* talks to Dan Smith, who works in disaster mitigation for a government agency.

2 'Dan, could you tell us what disaster mitigation means?'

'Disaster mitigation means attempting to minimize the impact of natural disasters both before and after they happen. My department and I work in two specific areas to try and do this: risk **reduction** and risk analysis. Both are **crucial** in disaster mitigation.'

3 'What do you mean by risk reduction?'

'Risk reduction means many things. It is not just referring to big engineering projects like dams. Often, small **community** projects can be the most effective means of risk reduction. The main way floods can be prevented is by the construction and **maintenance** of earth-wall defences, called levees. These block the progress of rising water. However, even the best levees can't protect against the **devastating** power of a tsunami. In this case, early-warning systems are lifesavers. They can let people know as early as possible if there is likely to be flooding.'

4 'What types of risk analysis do you do?'

'Firstly, risk analysis concerns flood mapping, where we **identify** the parts of the country which are at most risk from flooding. Secondly, there is mitigation planning, which helps local communities plan for when disaster strikes. Thirdly, we make sure that the country's dams all work properly and are safe. Although many people **criticize** dams because of their environmental impact, they also have many benefits such as hydroelectricity, irrigation, water storage, water sports and, of course, flood control. In terms of a cost-benefit analysis, we are definitely ahead.'

5 'Do you think countries are better prepared now for natural disasters than they were in the past?'

'Definitely. We are constantly developing new flood-prevention solutions. Some examples of these kinds of **measures** include the construction of sea walls and bulkheads[2], which protect the coasts, and the redesign of power stations and subway tunnels in the New York City area after the devastating damage caused by Hurricane Sandy in 2012. In the UK, another good example is the Thames Barrier, a huge engineering project designed to prevent London from flooding.'

6 'Aren't programmes like that very expensive? What lower-cost alternatives are there?'

'Flood prevention does not have to be expensive. Sandbags, for example, can be a highly effective way of stopping flood water.'

7 'Is there any more that can be done, or are we as prepared as we can be?'

'There's always more that could be done. But remember that the government can only be responsible for flood prevention up to a certain point. People have to become aware of the dangers of flooding themselves. This is crucial. Expensive early-warning systems are a waste of money if people pay no attention to them.'

[1]**illuminating** (adj) giving you new information about a subject
[2]**bulkhead** (n) an underwater wall

WHILE READING

4 Read the interview again. Write *T* (true), *F* (false) or *DNS* (does not say) next to the statements. Correct the false statements.

_____ **1** Dan Smith works for an international organization.
_____ **2** Risk reduction and risk analysis are both important parts of disaster mitigation.
_____ **3** Large-scale projects are always effective for risk reduction.
_____ **4** Planning for natural disasters has improved in recent years.
_____ **5** The New York City subway tunnel redesign cost $20 million.
_____ **6** Low-technology solutions can protect against flooding, too.

5 Answer the following questions based on the text.

1 What is the function of *disaster mitigation*?
2 What is a synonym phrase for a *levee*?
3 Why do some people criticize dams?
4 Who is responsible for flood prevention?

Identifying cohesive devices

SKILLS

Good academic writing flows easily and is not too repetitive. The writer needs to show links between ideas without repeating the same words. Using pronouns and synonyms in the place of nouns and noun phrases can help. To read well in English, you need to be able to identify what these pronouns and synonyms refer to.

*Flooding is happening more frequently and knowing how to tackle this **natural disaster** has become vital. Here the writer uses the synonym 'natural disaster' not to repeat the word flooding.*
Earthquakes are very common in **Japan. This country** has approximately 1, 500 earthquakes a year.

In order to avoid repetition the writer refers back to Japan using the pronoun 'this country'.

6 Find these words and phrases underlined in the interview. Write the nouns or noun phrases that they refer to.

1 two specific areas _____
2 It _____
3 These _____
4 this case _____
5 these kinds of measures _____
6 that _____
7 them _____

READING BETWEEN THE LINES

7 Work with a partner. Which of the opinions do you think Dan Smith would agree with?

1 It's the government's responsibility to protect us from natural disasters.
2 Surely it's more important to spend time and money on ways to stop water from causing floods, rather than finding out which areas are likely to flood. We already know that.
3 Dams are more trouble than they're worth.
4 Building sea walls is a waste of money – sandbags are just as good.
5 People in flood-risk areas need to be educated about the risks and about how they can help themselves.

DISCUSSION

8 Work with a partner. Discuss the questions.

1 Does your country ever have problems with flooding? If so, how do people protect themselves?
2 Which countries have particularly serious problems with flooding? Can you think of reasons why?

READING 2

PREPARING TO READ

1 You are going to read an article about Denmark, one of the most environmentally friendly countries in the world. Discuss the meaning of the words below with a partner and then complete the questions. Use a dictionary to help you.

> emission   drought   sustainability
> initiatives   awareness campaign   innovation
> infrastructure   pioneers   greenhouse gases

1 What _____ does your country currently have in place to fuel electric cars?
2 Which countries do you think are _____ when it comes to being environmentally friendly?
3 What can companies do to improve environmental _____ ?
4 How can we all reduce harmful carbon _____ ?

5 What _____ has your government put in place to tackle climate change?

6 In some parts of the world a lack of water is common. Have you ever had a _____ in your country?

7 Educating people about environmental issues is important. What _____ can the government provide which would be most useful?

8 Many countries are thinking of new ideas to solve the issue of climate change. Can you think of any recent _____ which have helped preserve the environment?

9 As a result of _____ being released into the air, the earth is getting warmer. Has the temperature increased in your country or places you know?

2 Check your answers to Exercise 1 with a partner. Then discuss your answers to the questions.

3 Look at the pictures showing a map of Denmark and its capital city, Copenhagen. Discuss the questions below with a partner.

PREDICTING CONTENT USING VISUALS

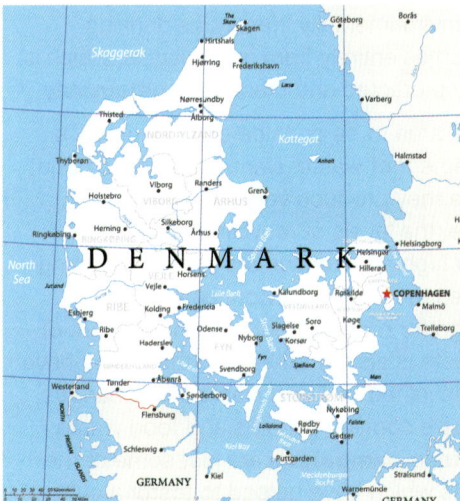

1 What surrounds Denmark? Because of its location what type of industry/energy do you think Denmark has?

2 What types of renewable energy might they have?

3 What form of transport can you see? Why do you think it is popular?

4 Work with a partner. Discuss the questions.

USING YOUR KNOWLEDGE

1 What type of initiatives do you think Denmark have invested in to make it one of the most environmentally friendly countries in the world?

2 What do you think the phrase 'going green' means?

GOING GREEN IN DENMARK

1 In today's world being environmentally friendly should be high on the agenda[1] for all countries. Every time a natural disaster such as flooding occurs, we are reminded of just what a fragile state our environment is in. Whilst many nations are indeed making great efforts to prevent the negative impacts of climate change there is a small group of countries which are really leading the way in terms of 'green' initiatives. Countries such as: Switzerland, Japan, Thailand and Denmark. In this article, we will consider Denmark's remarkable commitment to protecting the environment, as in 2022 it was ranked first in the Environmental Performance Index (EPI.

2 Historically, Denmark is a country based on agriculture and fishing, and therefore its connection to nature has always been strong. Perhaps this is the reason why the Danes have become **pioneers** at promoting sustainability and have made protecting the environment an integral part of their culture. The country has a long history of green **initiatives**. Through decades of sustained effort, the Danes have invested in: green transportation, renewable energy, water management and waste recycling.

3 One key way in which Denmark strives to protect the environment is by investing in and promoting cleaner modes of transport. Vehicles contribute significantly to CO_2 **emissions** and therefore this is a key area in which countries need to invest. Danes have therefore fostered a cycling culture and in Copenhagen it is said there are more bikes than cars. Denmark has provided its citizens with a complex network of green cycle routes, thus encouraging people to use their bikes instead of their cars. Vehicles are still prominent in Denmark, but cars which are of low or zero emission, are common. This is supported by the fact that there is a fuelling **infrastructure** in place for electric, hydrogen and natural gas vehicles.

4 Another key feature of Danish culture is their commitment to the use of renewable energy sources. By using cleaner forms of energy Denmark aims to reduce carbon emissions, and decrease the emission of **greenhouse gases**. In fact, Denmark aims to be free of fossil fuels by 2050 and rely solely on renewable energy sources such as wind, solar and geothermal[2] power.

Wind power has a particularly prominent place in Danish culture, and this began after the oil crisis in 1973, when investment in wind turbines became a necessity. Since then, the use of these turbines has become common, and the government has plans to construct one of the world's first energy islands. This initiative would utilize the abundant wind energy resources in the North and Baltic Seas. It is projected that these offshore wind turbines will have the capacity to power at least 5 million households.

5 Water management is another key global environmental challenge the world faces. **Droughts** are becoming more prevalent, and more people than ever are struggling to get access to clean drinking water and sanitation[3]. However, this is certainly not the case in Denmark, which provides some of the cleanest tap water in the world. The way in which this is achieved is also environmentally friendly, as drinking water comes entirely from groundwater, which is carefully protected and managed **sustainably**.

6 The final area to be considered is Denmark's management of waste. Danes take the amount of waste they produce very seriously. For example, the levels of recycling in Denmark are very high and consumers can use vending machines to return their bottles and cans in exchange for money. Reducing the amount of food waste is also another area the Danes have heavily invested in. Food waste supermarkets, food waste cooking schools and food waste **awareness campaigns** are just some of the initiatives which have helped to foster a culture which prioritizes a reduction in food waste.

7 Whilst no country can be regarded as the winner in the fight against climate change, it is important to recognize those nations who are using **innovation** to rethink the way we do things, in order to protect and preserve our environment for future generations. Denmark is without doubt one of those pioneers and it would be neglectful of other countries not to follow suit with some of its green initiatives.

[1]**agenda** (n) important subjects that have to be dealt with
[2]**geothermal** (adj) of or connected with the heat inside the earth
[3]**sanitation** (n) a system of protecting people's health by removing dirt and waste

WHILE READING

5 Read the article quickly for the main ideas. Underline the key points in each paragraph (the first paragraph has been done for you). Compare your answers with a partner.

READING FOR MAIN IDEAS

6 Read the article again find the answers to the following questions:

1 According to the writer, why has Denmark always been committed to protecting the environment?

_____

2 How has the government encouraged its citizens to use bicycles?

_____

3 What ambitions does Denmark have with regard to the use of renewable energy sources in the future?

_____

4 Where does the tap water come from in Denmark and how is it so clean?

_____

5 How much electricity is projected to be generated by the offshore wind turbines which surround Denmark's planned energy islands?

_____

READING FOR DETAIL

READING BETWEEN THE LINES

7 Work with partner and discuss the following questions.

1 Why did an investment in wind turbines become a necessity for Denmark?

_____

2 Why do you think levels of recycling cans and bottles are high in Denmark?

_____

3 Why does the writer say, 'no country can be regarded as the winner in the fight against climate change'?

_____

MAKING INFERENCES

DISCUSSION

SYNTHESIZING

8 Work with a partner. Use ideas from Reading 1 and Reading 2 to discuss the questions.

1 Denmark is a relatively small country. Do you think being environmentally friendly is more challenging for bigger countries? Why / Why not?
2 Which of the initiatives mentioned in Reading 2 are present in your country?

WRITING

9 Write about one of the following: transport, energy sources, waste management or water management. Write one paragraph for each of the questions below.

1 What does your country currently do to be environmentally friendly in this area?
2 What more could they do?

⊙ LANGUAGE DEVELOPMENT

ACADEMIC NOUN PHRASES

VOCABULARY

Two or **three nouns** may sometimes be combined in academic writing in order to create a more **complex noun phrase** which **gives greater detail about the subject**. This is called a **compound noun.**

risk + analysis = risk analysis
risk + analysis + project = risk analysis project
The meaning of each noun usually remains the same.

risk = danger
analysis = looking at something in detail
project = a piece of work with a particular focus
risk analysis project = a piece of work which looks at dangers or threats in detail
When creating compound nouns, it may be necessary to make a noun out of adjectives, verbs or adverbs.

manufacture the product = product manufacturing

1 Work with a partner. Look at the words in the circle below and try and make as many complex noun phrases as possible. *Remember you will need to change the adjectives and verbs into nouns.*

Example: *disaster mitigation*

disaster (n)   polluted (adj)   carbon (n)

habitat (n)   lanes (n)   fires (n)

emissions (n)   household   (n)   climate (n)

mitigate (v)   change (n)   cycle (n)

lose (v)   waste (n)   air (n)   forest (n)

NATURAL DISASTER VOCABULARY

2 Look at the adjective-noun collocations. Circle the collocation in each group which is correct.

1 A *significant / big / major* disaster occured.
2 A(n) *big / severe / uncontrollable* fire destroyed the area.
3 It spread through *full / highly populated / attractive* resorts in Greece today.
4 Many people were forced to abandon their *comfortable / affordable / special* accommodation and escape to the sea.
5 The cause of this *bad / devastating / unhappy* incident is currently unknown.
6 Some experts believe it was arson, whilst others think it was the *major / great / extreme* temperatures which caused the wildfires.

3 Imagine you are a newspaper reporter and you have been asked to write a report on an incident of wildfires. Use the collocations above to write your article. Write about 100 words.

Remember that when you write a newspaper article your language needs to be formal and the passive tense is often used.

WRITING

CRITICAL THINKING

At the end of this unit, you are going to write a problem–solution essay. Look at this unit's writing task below.

> Choose a case study of a natural disaster. Write an essay about the problems it caused and provide both short and long-term solutions, taking cost into consideration. Write 350–400 words.

ANALYZE

1 Read the two case studies. Match strategies (1–9) to case studies (A–B). Each strategy may be applied to one or both case studies.

Case study A: Wildfire risk

Location: Southern Australia
Geography: heavily forested areas
Country GDP rank in world: #12
Potential causes of fire: drought, arson[1], global warming
Human consequences: 1–5 deaths per year
Frequency: common during summer months
Effects: loss of life, destruction of homes and other buildings; destruction of habitats for wild animals; pollution from smoke
Short-term solutions: better law enforcement against arson, establishing volunteer fire groups (£0 per year); using satellite images and drone aircrafts to detect and follow fires (£15,000 per year)
Long-term solution: Government restrictions against building in hot, dry areas (£0 per year)

[1]**arson** (n) the crime of intentionally starting a fire in order to damage or destroy something

Case study B: Dust storms

Location: Mauritania, North Africa
Geography: mainly desert
Country GDP rank in world: #154
Potential causes: wind, drought, farming practices, deforestation
Human consequences: difficult to measure, as fatal consequences are not always immediate
Frequency: until early 1960s about two per year; since 1960s, 80 per year
Effects: loss of fertile soil; health dangers (breathing problems); poor visibility for transport
Short-term solutions: force better farming practices in the country such as crop rotation (£0 per year); stop deforestation (national income loss approx. £25,000 per year)
Long-term solutions: improved national irrigation systems (£500,000 per year); set up more clinics to treat people with asthma and other health problems (£7 million per year)

STRATEGIES CASE STUDIES

1 Stopping deforestation _____
2 Educating the community about prevention and protection

   _____

3 Setting up more clinics to treat sick people _____
4 Increasing law enforcement against arson _____
5 Establishing volunteer groups _____
6 Improving irrigation systems _____
7 Restricting the areas where building is allowed _____
8 Encouraging responsible farming practices _____
9 Developing monitoring systems via satellites and drones

   _____

SKILLS

Evaluating arguments

When you need to evaluate arguments against two different criteria simultaneously, a diagram like the one below is a very effective tool. At each end of the x-axis and the y-axis, add opposing factors. Then place the argument at the relevant point (e.g. in the top-right section if expensive and long-term; in the bottom-left if inexpensive and short-term).

2 **Now read the case studies again and place the preventive strategies from Exercise 1 in the diagram.**

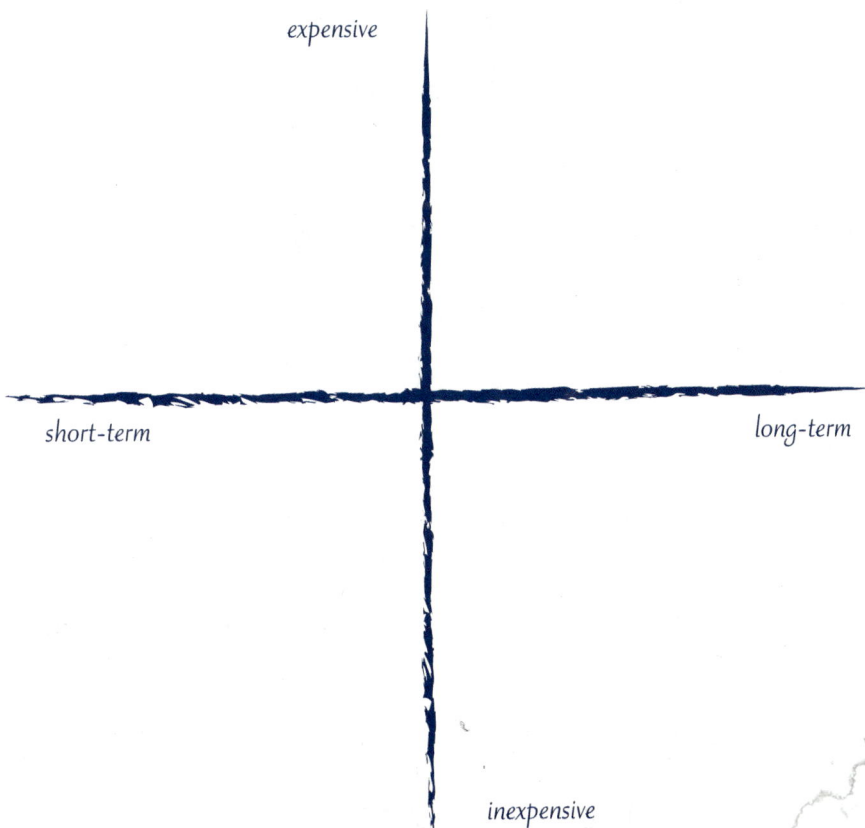

EVALUATE

```
                    expensive
                        |
                        |
                        |
                        |
    short-term ─────────┼───────── long-term
                        |
                        |
                        |
                    inexpensive
```

3 Answer the following questions. Assume that there is a developing country which sometimes has wildfires or dust storms, but which is not currently following any of the strategies mentioned in the case studies.

1 Which measures would be easiest to take? Which would be hardest?

_____

_____

2 Can you think of any other measures not mentioned in the case studies?

_____

_____

3 Choose the three best solutions to recommend to each country.

_____

_____

4 Compare your answers with a partner. Make any changes to your answers in Exercise 3 based on any good suggestions you hear.

GRAMMAR FOR WRITING

EXPRESSING SOLUTIONS USING *IT*

Most sentences in English need a **subject** as well as a **verb**.

Minimizing the risks caused by natural disasters is possible.

The words in bold are the subject. **When the subject is long like this**, it sounds better to change the sentence, so we **use it as the subject**.

It is possible to minimize the risks caused by natural disasters.

Note that *it* has no meaning in this structure. It is only included to provide a subject for the sentence.

There are a number of grammar patterns which follow *it*.

1 *it + is +* noun phrase or adjective + infinitive

It is a good idea to keep an emergency kit at home.

It is important to prepare for natural disasters.

2 *it + is +* adjective + gerund

It is worth preparing for natural disasters.

3 *it + is +* noun phrase or adjective + *that* + clause

It is surprising that governments do not always prepare for disasters.

It is a sad fact that many lives were lost.

1 The sentence halves in the first column are commonly used phrases in writing. Match the sentence halves. In some cases, more than one answer may be possible.

1 It is important
2 It is unlikely
3 It can be difficult
4 It is worth
5 It is not worth
6 It is never a good idea to
7 It is not surprising
8 It is not easy to

a preparing for droughts even during the rainy season.
b to protect homes and businesses from floods.
c to guarantee flood protection in areas close to major rivers.
d that a tsunami can overcome large-scale flood defences.
e build homes in a flood zone.
f that short-term drought solutions will work over a long period.
g persuade people to move away from areas at risk of floods.
h investing in tsunami warnings if people don't pay attention to them.

2 Complete the sentences with your own ideas about the environment. Give reasons.

Example: *It is important to recycle as much as possible because we need to conserve natural resources.*

1 It is never a good idea to

_____.

2 It is worth

_____.

3 It can be difficult

_____.

4 It is not surprising

_____.

5 It is not easy to

_____.

3 Compare your answers with a partner. Do you agree or disagree with their statements?

ACADEMIC WRITING SKILLS

DEVELOPING IDEAS

SKILLS

A body paragraph which supports a thesis statement must give reasons why the thesis is valid by providing examples. These examples need to be sequenced in a logical way. The presentation of ideas in a body paragraph needs to be cohesive – it needs to 'flow' well, and the connection of ideas should be clear to the reader. End a body paragraph with a sentence that gives the idea a 'finished' feeling.

1 **Number the sentences to create a body paragraph that flows logically. Then re-write the paragraph in the correct order.**

a It can take firefighters days, even weeks to put these fires out.

_____

b Although one would expect people to try and protect the environment, carelessness can often lead to disaster.

_____

c Therefore, the next time we light a campfire or use fireworks we should be very mindful of our actions.

_____

d Once these fires are irresponsibly started, they can burn through acres of land in a matter of hours.

_____

e Unfortunately, humans are often the leading cause of wildfires.

_____

f For example, an unattended campfire, cigarette or firework can easily become out of control especially in windy conditions.

_____

PARALLEL STRUCTURE

SKILLS

Parallel structure means using the same pattern of words to show that ideas have the same level of importance. These ideas are connected with conjunctions such as 'and'.

In order to protect the environment, we should all be **recycling**, **saving water** and **using bicycles more**.
In this example, **the verb + _ing_** is used to stress the importance of each idea.
If we said the sentence below, the impact would be less effective.

X . . . . we should all be recycling, saving water and we need to use our bicycles more.

2 Read the sentences. Correct the words or phrases which do not have parallel structure.

1 People can learn about approaching storms from the regular media, social media sites, or talk to their friends and neighbours.

2 In places like Kenya, residents can prepare for droughts by recycling water, building wells and they should establish desalination plants.

3 Dan Smith is a specialist in disaster mitigation, risk reduction and he analyzes risk.

4 Severe storms can be very scary, seriously damaging and the expense is surprising.

5 Common examples of natural disasters include earthquakes, floods and typhoons can also occur.

3 Finish these sentences with an appropriate parallel structure phrase.

1 We should keep many things in our homes to stay safe during a storm, such as bottled water,

_____ .

2 When a tsunami occurs, it can damage buildings and

_____ .

3 There are several strategies that Australia can use to prepare for wildfires, such as monitoring the area with drones,

_____ .

WRITING TASK

Choose a case study of a natural disaster. Write an essay about the problems it caused and provide both short and long-term solutions, taking cost into consideration. Write 350–400 words.

1 Complete the following steps:

1 Choose a case study you are interested in. Perhaps one that you have been affected by or one have seen on the news. Or you can use one of the case studies from the **critical thinking section.**

2 Research your case study if needed and make notes and a diagram as shown on page 95. Think of at least three solutions – one short-term and two long-term.

2 Work with a partner. Discuss how you will structure your essay and which points you will include.

3 Now write your plan.

4 Refer to the Task checklist on page 100 as you prepare your essay.

WRITE A FIRST DRAFT

5 Complete the essay using your outline.

REVISE

6 Use the Task checklist to review your essay for content and
   structure.

TASK CHECKLIST	✔
Did you use an appropriate structure for the essay?	
Do your paragraphs all include topic sentences and the development of ideas?	
Did you identify both short- and long-term solutions in your essay?	
Did you include relevant supporting information in the essay?	
Did you make sure all of your sentences contain parallel structure?	
Did you refer to a case study?	
Did you check the word count?	

7 Make any necessary changes to your essay.

EDIT

8 Use the Language checklist to edit your essay for language errors.

LANGUAGE CHECKLIST	✔
Did you use academic noun phrases where appropriate?	
Did you check that the words in your phrases collocate correctly?	
Did you correctly use phrases with *it*, where appropriate?	
Did you spell any environmental collocations correctly?	

9 Make any necessary changes to your essay.

OBJECTIVES REVIEW

1 Check your learning objectives for this unit. Write *3*, *2* or *1* for each objective.

3 = very well   2 = well   1 = not so well

I can …

watch and understand a video about population and water. _____

identify cohesive devices. _____

analyze a case study. _____

evaluate arguments. _____

express solutions using *it*. _____

develop ideas. _____

use parallel structure. _____

write a problem-solution essay. _____

2 Use the *Unlock* Digital Workbook for more practice with this unit's learning objectives.

UNLOCK
**DIGITAL
WORKBOOK**

WORDLIST

criticize (v) ◎	identify (v) ◎	policy (n) ◎
crucial (adj)	issue (n) ◎	reduction (n) ◎
devastating (adj)	large-scale (adj) ◎	rely on (phr v)
disaster (n) ◎	long-term ◎	severe (adj)
emission (n) ◎	maintenance (n) ◎	strategy (n) ◎
extreme (adj) ◎	major (adj)	sustainability (n) ◎
greenhouse gas (n) ◎	measure (n) ◎	

◎ = high-frequency words in the Cambridge Academic Corpus

UNIT 5

ARCHITECTURE

LEARNING OBJECTIVES

Watch and listen
Watch and understand a video about government grants for energy-efficient homes.

Reading skill
Skim a text.

Critical thinking
Create a persuasive argument.

Grammar
Use correct register in academic writing.

Academic writing skill
Order information; prioritize arguments.

Writing task
Write a persuasive essay.

UNL⌀CK YOUR KNOWLEDGE

Work with a partner. Discuss the questions.

1 Look at the photo. Which style of building in the picture do you like the most? Why?

2 Do you prefer older buildings or more modern architecture? Why?

3 Which are the most beautiful buildings in your country? Why?

4 Do you think it is important to protect old buildings? Why / Why not?

WATCH AND LISTEN

Gareth Redmond-King
Head of Climate & Energy, World Wide Fund for Nature

PREPARING TO WATCH

ACTIVATING YOUR KNOWLEDGE

1 Work with a partner and answer the questions.

1 How can people save energy in their homes?

2 How can the government encourage people to save energy at home?

PREDICTING CONTENT USING VISUALS

2 Look at the pictures from the video. Discuss the questions with a partner.

1 What do you think the workers are doing in photos 1, 3 and 4?

2 What do you notice about the house in the last picture?

3 Do you think these homes are energy efficient? Why / Why not?

| GLOSSARY

insulation (n) covering that prevents heat, sound, or electricity from escaping

intense lobbying (n phr) a powerful effort to convince the government to do something

be a rarity (v) to be very unusual

the norm (n) the usual way that things happen

scrap (v) to not continue with a plan

set something back (phr v) to delay an event or process

WHILE WATCHING

UNDERSTANDING MAIN IDEAS

3 ▶ Watch the video. Write *T* (true) or *F* (false) next to the statements below. Correct the false statements.

_____ 1 Most homes in Britain are not very well insulated.

_____ 2 The government helps low-income home owners with the cost of insulation.

_____ 3 Builders are struggling to work out how to build more energy-efficient homes.

_____ 4 Housing developments with energy-efficient homes are uncommon in Britain.

4 ▶ Watch again. Complete the notes.

(1)_____ of the money that people in Britain spend on heating is wasted because their homes do not have enough (2)_____ . The government wants to change that, aiming for an 80% (3)_____ in emissions. Builders already know how to build (4)_____ homes. They can build homes that maintain a comfortable (5)_____ without using much energy. Nevertheless, the emissions rate in Britain is (6)_____ . Earlier, there was a (7)_____ standard for building homes, but after an intense lobbying effort, it was (8)_____ . Today, with no clear standard, builders are (9)_____ about what kind of homes they should build.

5 Work with a partner. Discuss the questions.

1 The 'passive-house standard' means that houses stay warm enough without extra heating. How do you think that works?
2 Why do you think there was 'intense lobbying' against the passive-house standard? Who do you think was lobbying against it?

DISCUSSION

6 Work with a partner and answer the questions.

1 Is the home you live in energy-efficient? Give some examples to support your answer.
2 Is your community concerned about energy efficiency? Give some examples.
3 What are some other major sources of carbon emissions outside of homes?

READING 1

PREPARING TO READ

1 You are going to read an article about 'green' buildings. Work with a partner. Answer the questions.

1 Is it important to build environmentally-friendly buildings?
2 How can architects design buildings that use less energy?
3 Are there many 'green' buildings in your country?

2 Match the definitions to the words in the box below.

> **conservation** (n) **durable** (adj) **efficiency** (n)
> **compromise** (n) **relevant** (adj) **second-hand** (adj) **sector** (n)

1 an agreement between two sides who have different opinions, in which each side gives up something it had wanted: _____
2 having been used in the past by someone else: _____
3 related to a subject or to something happening or being discussed _____
4 the protection of plants, animals and natural areas from the damaging effects of human activity _____
5 a part of society which can be separated from other parts because of its own special character _____
6 able to last a long time without being damaged _____
7 something that is done without wasting time, energy or money: _____

3 In pairs, complete the sentences below with one of the words in the box above.

1 Buildings which are tough and last a long time are usually made from _____ materials.
2 The city planning committee may have to make a(n) _____ in order to both save money and use high-quality building materials.
3 It is important for developers to consider the _____ of their plan so that they avoid wasting time, money or labour.
4 Developers cannot build in certain locations, such as rainforests, due to environmental _____ .
5 If previously used wood is still in good condition, a builder may choose to use it for construction even though it is _____ .
6 Most architects work in the private _____ , which means they work for companies and not for the government.
7 The architect who designed the building does not think people's opinion of its appearance is _____ to its purpose.

Skimming a text

Skimming is reading a text quickly in order to get a general idea of its main points. It is particularly useful when you have a great deal of information to read in a short space of time, or when it is not necessary to understand a text in detail. Readers often skim a text to find out if it will be useful or not before reading it more thoroughly. This is particularly important in academic reading where you may only have time to read the most useful information.

Do …

✔ look at the title, any subheadings and illustrations – they will often give clues about the content.

✔ read the introductory paragraph, which should tell you what the text will be about.

✔ read the concluding paragraph.

✔ read the first sentence of each paragraph, which may present its topic.

Don't …

✗ stop to look up unknown words.

✗ say the individual words that you read in your head. Try to just focus on the meaning.

✗ read examples.

SKIMMING

4 Look at the photos with the article on page 108. Read only the title, the introductory paragraph and the concluding paragraph. Complete the statement below.

This article will be useful for a student who needs to find out about …

a houses in New Mexico.

b the causes of climate change.

c the conservation of ancient buildings.

d arguments for ecologically responsible construction.

5 How did you find the answer for Exercise 3? What was most helpful – the photos, the title, the introductory paragraph or the concluding paragraph?

6 Skim the article and write the corresponding paragraph numbers next to the ideas below. Then check your answers with a partner.

a a type of eco-building _____

b a specific example of an eco-home _____

c a current trend in construction _____

d the need to produce eco-buildings _____

e the pros and cons of producing eco-buildings _____

f an example of a public eco-building _____

We need more green buildings

1   In recent years, there has been a general trend for new buildings to be more environmentally friendly, or more 'green'. Such a building is sometimes called an eco-building. These buildings use energy and water efficiently, which reduces waste and pollution. However, installing features like solar panels and water-recycling systems involves higher construction costs than in a traditional building. Despite these extra costs, green buildings are good for the planet and their benefits are clear.

2   In New Mexico, in the US, there are homes called Earthship houses, constructed from recycled bottles, tyres, aluminium cans and other garbage. Often the cans, bottles and tyres are filled with soil and then the outsides are covered with natural mud. These homes are designed to use solar power – the energy from the sun – rather than electricity produced from fossil fuels[1]. These recycled-construction designs are just as **relevant** for other types of buildings. In both Uruguay and Sierra Leone, for example, there are recycled-construction schools for local children.

3   In the UAE, the Zulekha Hospital in Sharjah was the first Middle Eastern building to be awarded 'platinum certification' by the Green Building Council. They received this by meeting various green requirements, including sustainability, water and energy efficiency and indoor environmental quality. The hospital executives researched ways to make the hospital green during the construction phase of the building, and numerous features were put into the design to make it sustainable and show their commitment to the environment.

4   Another example of an eco-building is a private residence in Wales known as the 'Hobbit House'. Its frame is made of wood and the walls are made of straw, which provides excellent insulation. The roof consists of mud planted with grass, which keeps heat in and has a low impact on the environment. Solar panels provide electricity for lighting and electrical equipment. Water is supplied directly from a nearby river and is also collected from the roof for use in the garden, avoiding the need to waste clean water. Low-impact houses like this one are green because they use **second-hand** materials and do not rely on fossil fuels, but instead use renewable energy sources such as solar or wind power.

5   Critics of these kinds of eco-buildings say that while they may be good for the environment, there are practical problems with their affordability. They are often too costly to become a large-volume method of construction. There are further concerns over their long-term **efficiency**. Not much energy can be realistically generated by solar panels in places which do not have large amounts of sunlight, and not every location has access to a natural water source. However, overall, green buildings are worth it. Yet, in order to finance environmentally friendly construction and produce an affordable building, **compromises** have to be made. These may be that the building will have to be smaller or made of less **durable** materials and with technology which uses more energy. Perhaps these compromises are easier to make for schools, where ideas about **conservation** are useful for education, or for businesses where ecologically aware features are a useful marketing tool, rather than for private homes.

6   The argument for constructing green buildings is clear. According to the United Nations, material resource use in the construction **sector** is expected to reach nearly 90 billion tonnes very soon, and may more than double by 2050. Without greater resource efficiency, sustainable development goals will not be reached. We need to be wise about how we use these resources for the good of the planet. However, it remains to be seen whether we are able to accept the financial and practical compromises of producing and living in environmentally friendly buildings.

[1]**fossil fuels** (n) fuels such as gas, coal and oil produced in the earth from the remains of plants and animals

WHILE READING

7 Read the article. Write *RC* (recycled-construction building), *HH* (Hobbit House) or *N* (neither type of building) for the architectural features below.

1 a grass roof _____
2 a local water source _____
3 recycled cans and bottles _____
4 gas heating _____
5 a wooden construction _____
6 straw walls _____
7 recycled tyres _____
8 natural insulation _____

8 Read the article again. Write *T* (true), *F* (false) or *DNS* (does not say) next to the statements. Then correct the false statements.

_____ 1 Generally, eco-buildings are becoming more popular.
_____ 2 Eco-buildings cost double the price of a traditional building.
_____ 3 Environmentally friendly practices are relevant, no matter what size of building you are constructing.
_____ 4 Some old construction methods can be useful in environmentally friendly construction.
_____ 5 Fossil fuels are examples of renewable types of energy.
_____ 6 Some schools are eco-friendly buildings.
_____ 7 The United Nations produces data about global energy use.

READING BETWEEN THE LINES

9 Work with a partner. Answer the questions.

1 In the introduction, it is stated that 'the benefits are clear'. What do you think those benefits are?
2 Why do you think it was necessary for the Zulekha Hospital in Sharjah to consider green features during the construction phase, rather than later on?
3 How do you think recycled-construction schools might be effective educational aids for the students who attend them?

DISCUSSION

10 Work with a partner. Discuss the questions.

1 Would you live in an eco-home if you had to pay more for its environmentally friendly features? Why / Why not?
2 How can we make our homes more environmentally friendly?

READING 2

PREPARING TO READ

1 You are going to read an essay on form and function in building design. In pairs discuss the meaning of the words in bold and then answer the questions. Use a dictionary to help you.

1 Which is more important for a building: its beauty or its **function**?

2 Some people believe that the building you are in can affect your mood. Which environments make you happy and which do you find **depressing**?

3 Have you even seen a building or a piece of architecture which you thought was **inspiring**?

4 Do you think that our homes **reflect** our personality? In what ways?

5 Do you know of any towns or cities which have a **reputation** for striking architecture?

6 Do you think beautiful and well-constructed buildings are a symbol of a **civilized** society?

7 Have you ever visited a place which **demonstrates** a wide variety of architectural styles?

2 Work with a partner. Discuss the questions.

1 Do you know of any buildings which look good but are not practical? For example, some old houses may look picturesque, but they can be difficult to maintain or expensive to heat.

2 Do you know of any buildings which are very functional, but you don't like the way they look?

3 Do you think that way your house looks is more important than how practical it is? Or are these two factors equally important?

3 Skim the essay opposite. Does the writer think it is more important to design a building which is beautiful or one which is functional?

BUILDING DESIGN: form vs function

1 At the start of the twentieth century, Louis Sullivan, one of the creators of modern architecture, said that 'form follows **function**'. The term 'functionalism' is used to describe the idea behind architecture which primarily focuses on the purpose of a building. However, many people disagree with this and feel that beauty is a more important factor in architectural design. In the modern world, it seems that most architects try to combine both ideas, aiming to create buildings which are both functional and **inspiring** in their beauty.

2 The reason for creating a building in the first place – its use – is clearly very important. When building an airport terminal, for example, you need to think of the needs of passengers as well as planes. Passengers want to get to their plane as quickly as they can, and planes need to be parked in a way which maximizes their ease of use. As such, many airport terminals have a circular shape with satellite areas. Residential homes need to have enough space for a family, art galleries need wall space to show pictures and factories need to produce goods as efficiently as possible. Each type of building has a different function, and, therefore, it has a different form.

3 On the other hand, many people believe that architects have a wider responsibility to society than just designing functional buildings. Beautiful, well-constructed buildings are a symbol of a **civilized** society and they **reflect** well **on** a business or the **reputation** of the owner. Ugly public buildings, however, can project a negative image of the organization. People say that living or working in an ugly place creates a **depressing** and uninspiring environment. In contrast, an attractive building can make people feel happier and increase their motivation to work.

4 In theory, there seems to be no reason why architecture cannot be both functional and beautiful. Yet in practice, this can cause problems. The Modern International style of the 1920s and 1930s, an example of which is the Guggenheim Museum in New York, was supposed to combine beauty with function. Many consider the museum's white spiral ramp beautiful, but there have been complaints that it is impractical, as it is difficult to stand back to view the art. Also, the ramp is so narrow that it can become overcrowded. The Farnsworth House by Ludwig Mies van der Rohe is another icon of beautiful design which **demonstrates** the idea that 'less is more'. However, critics have attacked it for a lack of privacy because of the huge glass windows. It also has a leaky flat roof and has been repeatedly flooded. It seems that even these two celebrated designs have problems with functionality.

5 If architects focus only on function, buildings may be cold, ugly and uninteresting. There is no doubt that a building with a beautiful form is something we can all appreciate. On the other hand, if they focus only on making it look beautiful, the building may be completely impractical. Therefore, blending these two ideas is necessary to create the perfect piece of architecture.

4 Match the original sentences (1–5) from the text to the correct paraphrases (a–e).

Original sentences

1 Beautiful, well-constructed buildings are a symbol of a civilized society.
2 People say that living or working in an ugly place creates a depressing and uninspiring environment.
3 Many people believe that architects have a wider responsibility to society than just designing functional buildings.
4 It seems that even these two celebrated designs have problems with functionality.
5 Each type of building has a different function, and, therefore, it has a different form.

Paraphrases

_____ a Unattractive buildings can make people feel unhappy and bored.
_____ b Attractive, safe buildings represent a cultured society.
_____ c Every construction has a different purpose, and is therefore designed according to different criteria.
_____ d These famous buildings may have won awards, but they still do not always fulfil users' needs.
_____ e People who design buildings have a duty to the general public.

SUMMARIZING

5 Read the essay again and then write a summary of each paragraph. To help you do this, underline the key points in each paragraph and then paraphrase the sentences. An example has been done for you:

Paragraph 1

While some architecture values function over form, there is an opposing view that the beauty of a building is more important than its functionality. In practice, most architects strive for a combination of both ideas.

READING BETWEEN THE LINES

MAKING INFERENCES

6 Work with a partner. Answer the questions.

1 How could a well-constructed building reflect well on the reputation of the owner?

_____

2 Does the author think the way a building looks is more important than its function?

_____

3 The author describes Farnworth House as 'less is more'. From this description, what do you imagine this building to look like inside?

_____

DISCUSSION

SYNTHESIZING

7 Work with a partner. Use ideas from Reading 1 and Reading 2 to discuss the questions.

1 Would you like to live in an eco-home? Why / Why not?
2 Do you think the building you work or study in, has an impact on your motivation? Why / Why not?
3 Have you ever formed an opinion of an organization or business based on the building it is in?

WRITING

8 Write two paragraphs about the most interesting building you have visited, or you would like to visit. Use these question prompts to help you write your answer.

1 What does it look like from the outside and inside?
2 Why is it your favourite building?
3 What is the building used for?
4 Which has been given greater consideration; its form or function?

⦿ LANGUAGE DEVELOPMENT

ACADEMIC WORD FAMILIES

When you learn new words, you should also try to learn **all forms** of the word.

*Architects aim for a **combination** of beauty and functionality. (noun)*
*Architects should **combine** beauty and functionality. (verb)*
*The **combined** beauty and functionality make this a perfect building. (adjective)*
These words are all from the same word family.

1 Complete the word families in the table.

Noun	Verb	Adjective	Adverb
function, functionalism	function	functional	functionally
environment		(1) _____	(2) _____
(3) _____	(4) _____	depressing	(5) _____
responsibility		(6) _____	(7) _____
architect, (8) _____		(9) _____	(10) _____
(11) _____		(12) _____	efficiently

2 Complete the sentences with words from the table in Exercise 1.

1 It is important to consider the _____ impact of any new building on its natural surroundings.
2 _____ is an architectural system which believes that function is more important than beauty.
3 Environmentally-friendly buildings usually use energy very _____ .
4 Architects need to plan buildings _____ in order to ensure that they are sustainable.
5 I find small dark rooms _____ to work in.

3 Now create your own sentences using the words in the table. You can use any form of the word you want.

ARCHITECTURE AND PLANNING VOCABULARY

4 Work in pairs. Match the words with their definitions. Use the Glossary on pages 196–198 to help you.

1 amenities	a tall buildings
2 green belts	b the area outside a city
3 outskirts	c the neighbourhood outside a city
4 skyscrapers	d facilities
5 structural engineer	e the countryside outside a city, which can't be built on
6 suburbs	f the spread of a city in the surrounding area
7 urban sprawl	g person who looks at how a building is constructed

5 Read the following sentences and decide whether you agree or disagree with each of these statements. Write your answers and then discuss them with a partner.

Remember to give reasons for your answers.

1 I would love to live or work in a **skyscraper**.

I strongly disagree with this statement, I don't think I would like it, as I hate heights. It just wouldn't be my ideal working environment.

2 Living in the **outskirts** of a city is far better than living in the very centre.

3 I would prefer to be an architect rather than a **structural engineer**.

4 When choosing an area to live in, the **amenities** it has are very important.

5 Having areas known as **'green belts'** is a good idea.

6 There is nothing wrong with **urban sprawl**, we need the space to build more houses.

7 Living in the **suburbs** is better than living in the city centre.

WRITING

CRITICAL THINKING

At the end of this unit, you will write a persuasive essay. Look at this unit's writing task below.

> Which is more important when building or buying a new home: its location or its size?

SKILLS

Creating a persuasive argument

To make the argument of your essay as persuasive as possible, focus on your most convincing points, and make sure they are supported with reliable and relevant evidence.

ANALYZE

1 Look at Reading 2 again. Using the information there, plus your own ideas, write down in the T-chart the advantages of focusing on either the beauty or the function of a building.

Advantages of focusing on beauty	Advantages of focusing on function
Beautiful buildings can put us in a good mood.	

EVALUATE

2 In each column, which idea is the most persuasive? Which idea is the least persuasive?

ANALYZE

3 Now look at the Writing task. With a partner, discuss the advantages of focusing on location and the advantages of focusing on size when planning a new building. Write notes in the T-chart below.

Advantages of focusing on location	Advantages of focusing on size

4 Highlight the ideas in your T-chart that you think are the most persuasive.

EVALUATE

GRAMMAR FOR WRITING

REGISTER IN ACADEMIC WRITING

GRAMMAR

Writing can either be **formal** or **informal** in style.

Informal writing tends to be similar to speaking. Informal English often includes:

- slang and colloquial expressions such as *cool*, *awesome* or *stuff*
- phrasal verbs (unless there is no alternative word)
- first-person personal pronouns (*I* and *me*)
- contractions such as *they're* instead of *they are*, or *it's* instead of *it is*
- the terms *a lot of* or *lots of*   • the terms *et cetera* or *etc.*
- exclamation marks (*!*)

Whereas **in formal written English**, writers usually use the following:

- longer, more complex sentences   • more precise, technical words
- more formal phrases and linking words

In academic writing you must use formal English.

1 Make the text below more formal by replacing the words in bold with the academic words and phrases from the box.

> challenging   in accommodation   be very costly   local amenities
> compact   However,   advantages of   are able to access
> socialize with friends   colleagues   alternatively   on the outskirts
> can afford   more spacious   the disadvantage   convenient
> In conclusion,   your priorities

Choosing the right place to live can be **super difficult!!** Living **somewhere** in the city centre can **cost an arm and a leg** and it can be **really really small**. **But,** the **good thing about** living in the centre is that you **can get to** all the **nearby places, like shops and restaurants**. This means it is probably easier for you to **hang out with your mates** and **people you work with**.

On the flip side, if you choose to live **out of the centre**, you probably **have enough money** to live in a place which is **bigger**. The **bad thing** about this though, is that it may not be **easy to get to the things you want easily**.

At the end of the day, it all depends on **what you think is important!**

GRAMMAR FOR WRITING   117

2 Rewrite the informal sentences below to make them sound more formal.

1 Doing up the house was a real uphill struggle.
2 The way the place looked was mind-blowing!
3 We are taking the plunge and getting our own place.
4 I like your new place because there is loads of room.

Compare your answers with a partner. Were they similar?

ACADEMIC WRITING SKILLS
ORDERING INFORMATION

SKILLS

To make writing fluent, academic writers often refer to the previous sentence when it has the same topic. Look at the examples:

When choosing a new house, the most important consideration may be location. **Areas near good schools** *are often popular.*

For many people the first criterion is **size. The number of bedrooms** *may be determined by family size.*

The beginning of the second sentence is a paraphrase of the end of the first one. Sometimes writers just use a reference word such as *this, that, these, those* or reference phrases like *That is why, For this reason* or *In spite of this.*

Some families prefer to expand their existing houses. **This** *allows all family members to live together.*

Living in a large city can mean parking problems. **In spite of this***, many people are drawn to urban areas.*

1 Write the phrases in the best places in the text.

> for this reason   in spite of this   it
> this combination   this profession

Architecture is often said to be a difficult subject to study.
(1)_____ , many people choose to go into (2)_____ . While some subjects are more quantitative, such as engineering, and others are more creative, such as art, architecture involves both.
(3)_____ may be what attracts people to (4)_____ as a career. Architects are in charge of creating the designs of all of the buildings we see every day. (5)_____ , they play an important role in our communities.

2 Complete the text using a word or phrase from the box below so that you can avoid repeating any of the words in bold.

> efficiency   new concepts   new technological development
> our impact on the environment
> properties equipped with various technologies   raw materials

Predicting architectural styles of the future is challenging, however, **some trends** are indeed emerging. These

(1)_____

include: **sustainable** architecture, 3D technology and smart homes. Housing which considers

(2)_____

is high on the agenda, as we are rapidly exhausting the earth's **natural resources**. These

(3)_____

can also be preserved by the development of **3D technology** in the construction industry. This is because this

(4)_____

streamlines the design and building process and therefore **reduces errors and waste**. Furthermore,

(5)_____

is the key focus of **smart homes**:

(6)_____

and systems that enhance convenience.

WRITING A PERSUASIVE ARGUMENT

SKILLS

Writers need to think about how to support a point of view by following it with specific facts or observations which can **persuade** the reader.

For example, this statement expressing a writer's point of view needs support in order to be persuasive:

It is important for us to continue to construct environmentally friendly buildings.

If the writer follows his or her point of view with the sentence below, it would not be very persuasive:

This is because they are good.

However, if the writer follows his or her point of view with the sentence below, it would be much more persuasive:

This is because they reduce carbon emissions, cause less harm to our environment and use fewer fossil fuels.

By saying that he or she thinks that something is good, the writer is just confirming his or her opinion. This is not especially persuasive. In contrast, offering facts as support for the argument appeals to the reader's sense of logic. This is a more persuasive technique.

3 Read the sentences in bold. Then decide which follow-up sentence sounds more persuasive.

1 **Small homes can be crowded.**
   a This lack of space can cause family tensions.
   b Larger houses mean everyone has more space

2 **Living in the suburbs is better than living in the city centre.**
   a It is usually cheaper to live in the suburbs and the environment is quieter and less congested.
   b Living in the suburbs is better because you can live more comfortably.

3 **Older architectural styles are more attractive than modern ones.**
   a Older architectural styles are more interesting to look at.
   b Older architectural styles often carry a sense of history, and they showcase fine craftsmanship.

4 **Ideally, we need homes which are convenient for travelling to work.**
   a This can save us valuable time and avoids the stress of being caught in heavy traffic.
   b It can be quicker to get to work.

4 Work in pairs. Imagine you are estate agents, and you are tasked with selling the two properties in the photos below. Student A should write a persuasive paragraph selling Property A and Student B should write a persuasive paragraph selling property B. Make sure you order information and write arguments using specific facts or information.

5 Compare your paragraphs. Which one is the more persuasive? Why?

WRITING TASK

Which is more important when building or buying a new home: its location or its size? Write 350–400 words.

1 You are going to write a persuasive essay. Look back at your notes in Critical thinking.

Discuss your ideas with a partner and then complete the plan below.

Paragraph 1: Introduction Introduce the topic / state your opinion / thesis statement	*Choosing where to live can be difficult and there are many factors to consider. This essay will argue that size is more important when choosing were to live.*
Paragraph 2: Persuasive Argument 1	
Paragraph 3: Persuasive Argument 2	
Paragraph 4: Conclusion	

2 Refer to the Task checklist on page 122 as you prepare your essay.

WRITE A FIRST DRAFT

3 Write your essay.

REVISE

4 Use the Task checklist to review your essay for content and structure.

TASK CHECKLIST	✔
Does your essay follow the structure provided?	
Are your arguments persuasive enough?	
Did you order information correctly?	
Do your examples adequately support your ideas?	

5 Make any necessary changes to your essay.

EDIT

6 Use the Language checklist to edit your essay for language errors.

LANGUAGE CHECKLIST	✔
Did you spell different words from the same word family correctly?	
Did you use subject-specific language correctly?	
Did you use formal academic language?	
Do references to subjects in previous sentences use pronouns correctly?	

7 Make any necessary changes to your essay.

OBJECTIVES REVIEW

8 Check your learning objectives for this unit. Write *3*, *2* or *1* for each objective.

3 = very well   2 = well   1 = not so well

I can ...

watch and understand a video about government grants
for energy-efficient homes.   _____

skim a text.   _____

create a persuasive argument.   _____

use correct register in academic writing.   _____

order information.   _____

prioritize arguments.   _____

write a persuasive essay.   _____

9 Use the *Unlock* Digital Workbook for more practice with this unit's
learning objectives.

UNL⊘CK
DIGITAL
WORKBOOK

WORDLIST

amenities (n)	durable (adj)	relevant (adj)
architectural (adj)	efficiency (n) ⊙	reputation (n) ⊙
architecturally (adv)	efficient (adj)	responsibility (n) ⊙
architecture (n) ⊙	environmental (adj)	responsible (adj)
civilized (adj)	environmentally (adv)	second-hand (adj)
compromise (n) ⊙	function (n) ⊙	sector (n) ⊙
conservation (n) ⊙	green belt (n phr)	skyscrapers (n)
demonstrate (v) ⊙	iconic (adj)	structural engineer
depress (v)	inspiring (adj)	(n phr)
depressing (adj)	outskirts (n)	suburban (adj)
depressingly (adv)	reflect on (phr v) ⊙	urban sprawl (n phr)
depression (n) ⊙		

⊙ = high-frequency words in the Cambridge Academic Corpus

ENERGY

UNIT 6

LEARNING OBJECTIVES

Watch and listen
Watch and understand a video about wind power.

Reading skill
Work out meaning from context.

Critical thinking
Evaluate benefits and drawbacks; organize ideas for an essay.

Grammar
Use defining and non-defining relative clauses.

Academic writing skill
Introduce advantages and disadvantages; make academic writing coherent.

Writing task
Write an advantages and disadvantages essay.

UNL⌀CK YOUR KNOWLEDGE

Work with a partner. Discuss the questions.

1 Look at the photo. What kind of energy is being used? Give reasons for your answer.

2 What problem is there with using fossil fuels?

3 What forms of energy do you think will be most popular in the future and why?

4 What problems might there be with renewable energy?

WATCH AND LISTEN

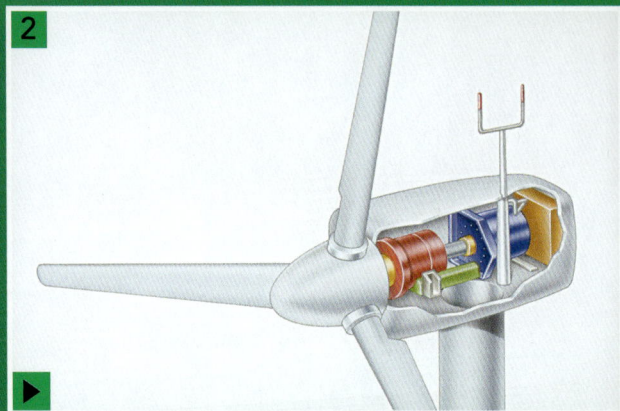

PREPARING TO WATCH

ACTIVATING YOUR KNOWLEDGE

1 Work with a partner. Which statements do you agree with?

1 Our society uses more energy than it did ten years ago.
2 There are many alternatives to fossil fuels.
3 Fossil fuels are the cheapest source of energy.
4 It is not a problem to depend on one main energy source.
5 Wind and solar power will be our future main sources of energy.

PREDICTING CONTENT USING VISUALS

2 Look at the pictures from the video. Discuss the questions with a partner.

1 What is the difference between the first and third pictures?
2 What does the second picture show?
3 Who do you think the person in the final picture is talking about?

GLOSSARY

renewable energy (n) energy that is produced using the sun, wind, etc., or from crops, rather than using fossil fuels such as oil or coal

overtake (v) to go past something by being larger or faster

smart technology (phr) smart technology uses computers and information in electronic form

continue unabated (v) to keep going without becoming weaker or less

WHILE WATCHING

UNDERSTANDING MAIN IDEAS

3 ▶ Watch the video. Write *T* (true), *F* (false) or *DNS* (does not say) next to the statements below. Correct the false statements.

_____ 1 Wind power provides almost 10% of the world's energy.
_____ 2 The UK gets more electricity from wind than from coal.
_____ 3 The UK's emission rates are decreasing.
_____ 4 Wind power is cheaper than traditional sources of energy.
_____ 5 Wind power presents some risks to health and safety.

4 ▶ Watch again. Write a supporting detail for each main idea.

1 Wind power is a good alternative to fossil fuels.

_____

2 The UK is an especially good place to develop wind power.

_____

3 In some ways, offshore wind power is preferable to onshore wind power.

_____

4 Wind power does have some disadvantages.

_____

UNDERSTANDING DETAIL

5 Work with a partner. Discuss the questions.

1 Why do you think there is widespread public support for this form of energy? Why is there also opposition?

2 Why does the energy analyst in the video claim that 'you won't find an energy analyst out there that disagrees' with a vision of the future that depends on renewables.

MAKING INFERENCES

DISCUSSION

6 Work with a partner and answer the questions.

1 Do you think a wind turbine near your home would be a good idea? Why / Why not?

2 Are there some places in the world that could benefit from wind power more than others?

3 Should communities have a choice about whether wind turbines are installed near them? Why / Why not?

READING 1

PREPARING TO READ

1 You are going to read an article on renewable energy. Match the types of renewable energy in the box to the photos (1–4) below.

> geothermal energy   hydropower   solar power   wind power

1 _____

2 _____

3 _____

4 _____

2 Read the sentences and match the bold words to definitions (a–g).

1 **Aquatic** creatures include fish, dolphins and whales.
2 Oil companies drill **offshore** to get petroleum from the sea floor.
3 Energy from the sun is considered an **inexhaustible** resource.
4 The **initial** response to the recycling programme has been good.
5 Waterfalls **generate** energy which we can use as power.
6 The need for energy sources for machines and appliances is **universal**.
7 Many people think that we need to **utilize** existing renewable energy sources such as solar and wind power.

a _____ (adj) at the beginning; first
b _____ (v) to cause to exist; produce
c _____ (adj) living in, happening in or connected with water
d _____ (adv) away from or at a distance from the land
e _____ (adj) existing everywhere or involving everyone
f _____ (v) to make use of something
g _____ (adj) in such large amounts that it cannot be used up

RENEWABLE ENERGY

HYDROPOWER

1 Hydropower is created when moving water turns turbines to create electricity. The source of the moving water can be rivers, waterfalls or the sea. Because flowing water continues to move, this creates an **inexhaustible** amount of energy which can be stored and used when the demand is highest. There are a few drawbacks, however. Water-powered turbines can have a negative environmental impact on **aquatic** wildlife and can endanger boats. Also, creating hydropower dams causes land behind the dams to permanently flood. Finally, it is expensive to set up hydropower systems – the average cost is between $1 million and $4 million.

WIND POWER

2 To create wind power, large turbines are placed on top of hills or **offshore**. The wind turns the blades, which **generate** energy. Wind turbines can be **utilized** on a large scale or on a small scale. Unlike hydropower, this process is relatively cheap and is considered one of the most affordable forms of electricity today. Also, it does not harm the air or land it uses. However, many people consider wind turbines ugly and noisy. Also, they rely on the wind, so if it is not windy, no energy is produced. Finally, like hydropower, wind turbines can be a threat to wildlife such as local birds.

SOLAR ENERGY

3 To use solar energy, solar panels absorb sunlight and, using devices called photovoltaic cells, turn it into electricity. The sun produces energy constantly, which makes solar energy an inexhaustible resource. Another benefit is that it generates no pollution. Solar energy can be adapted to work on a variety of buildings and in a variety of environments. However, a large area of land is needed to produce a large amount of solar power. Scientists have determined that if we wanted to try to power the entire Earth with renewable solar power, we would need to cover a land area about the size of Spain with solar panels. In places with less sunlight, solar power generation has limitations. Also, photovoltaic cells are fragile and can be easily damaged.

[1]**greenhouse gases** (n) gases, such as carbon dioxide, which cause a gradual warming of the Earth's atmosphere

BIOMASS ENERGY

4 Biomass is a biologically produced fuel made from plant and animal material, which is mostly composed of carbon, hydrogen and oxygen. It is the oldest source of renewable energy, used since humans first started burning wood for fire. Today, steam from burning biomass – made up of garbage and other organic waste, rather than wood – turns turbines, generating electricity. Biomass can re-grow over a relatively short period of time compared to the hundreds of millions of years that it takes for fossil fuels to form. It is also an efficient way to generate power, and it is **universal**. Another benefit is that it reduces the need to bury garbage under the ground in a landfill. However, some people are concerned that burning biomass contributes to global warming because it produces greenhouse gases[1]. Also, using biomass to generate energy on a large scale can be expensive.

GEOTHERMAL ENERGY

5 With geothermal energy, heat which is trapped in the ground can be converted into steam to turn turbines. The power it generates can then be used to produce electricity and heat buildings. Geothermal energy uses relatively simple technology. Like several of the other energy sources already mentioned, this process causes no pollution and is inexhaustible. The most active geothermal resources are usually found in areas near volcanoes or where geothermal activity naturally occurs. The largest area of this kind is known as the 'Ring of Fire'. It rims the Pacific Ocean and is bounded by eastern Asia and the western edge of the Americas. Outside of regions like these, geothermal energy is usually unavailable. The **initial** costs of installing a geothermal energy system are very high, but once it is built, the running costs are low.

GEOTHERMAL REGIONS OF THE WORLD

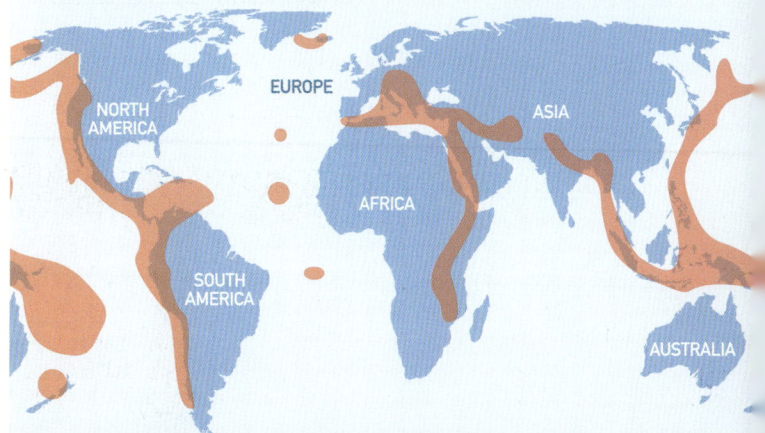

WHILE READING

3 Read the article and choose the best title.

    a 'Why are fossil fuels running out?'

    b 'The disadvantages of clean energy generation'

    c 'An overview of renewable energy production'

    d 'The benefits of renewable energy sources'

    e 'The pros and cons of environmental conservation'

4 Read the article again. Look at the statements below and decide if they are true or false. If you choose false, give reasons for your answer.

    1 Wind power is one of the most economical forms of renewable energy.

    2 There are no major drawbacks to using solar power as the resource is inexhaustible.

    3 The cost of installing and maintaining a geothermal energy system is very high.

    4 Biomass energy can be produced fairly quickly.

    5 The use of hydropower can be damaging to marine life.

5 Match each newspaper headline to a renewable energy source. Write the correct type of energy next to each headline.

    1 'Wave-power machines struggle in marine environment'
    _____

    2 'Rare eagle struck by newly constructed turbine' _____

    3 'Report shows 10,000 kg of waste used last year to fuel energy plant' _____

    4 'Amazing summer weather creates a huge supply of energy'
    _____

    5 'Government pledges millions for new plant near volcano'
    _____

    6 'Low rainfall suggests high electricity prices' _____

    7 'Environmentalists question the ability of this bio-energy source to renew itself' _____

READING BETWEEN THE LINES

Working out meaning from context

When you read a word you do not understand, you could look in a dictionary, but this will slow down your reading, and cause you to lose your place. Instead, try to guess the meaning from the context. Often you do not need the exact meaning of the word to be able to understand the sentence.

- Look at the surrounding words for meaning clues.

  *It is also an efficient way to **generate** power, and it is universal.*

- Try to substitute a word so that the sentence still makes sense.

  *The wind turns the blades, which **generate** (create) energy.*

- Look for a comparison or contrast between two sentence halves.

  *Water-powered turbines can have a negative environmental impact on aquatic wildlife and can **endanger** boats.*

- Use linking words or conjunctions to help you guess the meaning.

  *Although the government has **pledged** to build a new wind farm, some believe this will not happen.*

WORKING OUT MEANING

6 Read the article again and find the following words. See if you can identify their meaning, and highlight any other words in the text which helped you guess the meaning.

1 solar _____
2 fragile _____
3 stored _____
4 geothermal _____
5 wildlife _____
6 bury _____
7 bounded by _____

DISCUSSION

7 Work with a partner. Discuss the questions.

1 What is more important when considering energy use: cost or impact on the environment? Why?
2 Which types of renewable energy would be the most appropriate alternative to fossil fuels in your area?
3 Why might some people oppose the idea of having renewable energy farms in their area?

READING 2

PREPARING TO READ

1 You are going to read an essay on the advantages and disadvantages of electric cars. Read the words in bold in the essay and try to understand their meaning from the context. Match the words from the text (1–9) to the correct synonyms (a–i).

1 **drawbacks** (n)	a process of burning
2 **extreme** (adj)	b repair if needed
3 **unlike** (prep)	c produce something
4 **evidenced** (adj)	d disadvantages
5 **maintenance** (n)	e traditional
6 **manufacture** (v)	f different from
7 **conventional** (adj)	g not allow
8 **ban** (v)	h given proof
9 **combustion** (n)	i very great

2 Complete the following sentences with words from Exercise 1.

1 Some countries experienced _____ temperatures this summer.
2 There are many _____ to relying on fossil fuels, the most significant being the amount of pollution which is created.
3 _____ for your boiler can be costly, so it is a good idea to have insurance.
4 _____ sources of energy include oil, natural gas, coal and electricity. However, this is all set to change.
5 We need to _____ more electric cars to make them affordable for everyone.
6 In the future, it is possible that all governments will _____ the use of fossil fuels.
7 _____ fossil fuels, renewable energy sources are better for the environment.
8 Using renewable energy sources, such as solar power, significantly reduces levels of pollution, as _____ in China.

3 Now create your own sentences with these words from the text. You can use any form of the word you want.

*In order to **maintain** your car, it needs to be serviced regularly.*

4 Work in pairs and discuss the questions below.

1 What do you know about electric cars?

2 What do you think are the advantages and disadvantages of the electric car?

3 Do many people have electric cars in your area? Have you seen many charging points?

4 Would you buy an electric car? Why / Why not?

USING YOUR KNOWLEDGE

WHILE READING

5 Read the essay about the pros and cons of electric cars and then answer the questions below.

1 What does the writer say are the main advantages of electric cars?

_____

2 What are the main disadvantages of an electric car?

_____

3 What is the writer's final conclusion on this topic?

_____

READING FOR MAIN IDEAS

6 Work with a partner. Answer the questions.

1 What impact could a single electric vehicle have on levels of pollution?

_____

2 Why are EVs quieter than petrol fuelled cars?

_____

3 Why do EVs require less maintenance than conventional cars?

_____

4 Why are electric cars more expensive than petrol fuelled cars?

_____

5 How far can the most advanced electric cars travel?

_____

READING FOR DETAIL

THE PROS AND CONS OF THE ELECTRIC CAR

1 We are on the brink of[1] change for the car industry and countries around the world agree that all cars should be fuelled by an energy source which is more environmentally friendly, such as electricity. Essentially, an electric car is a vehicle powered by a battery, which is charged by an external electricity source. **Unlike** most current cars, which run on[2] fossil fuels, the electric car would not create **extreme** levels of pollution. However, despite this, many countries are delaying this switch to a greener energy source, because whilst this change would bring with it some enormous benefits, it also has some significant **drawbacks**. The following essay will consider both sides of the argument.

2 As already mentioned, perhaps the greatest advantage of electric vehicles (EVs), is that they are kinder to the environment. According to the Mayor of London, road pollution is currently responsible for half the city's air pollution. Unlike gasoline- or diesel[3]-fuelled cars, EVs produce zero exhaust pipe[4] emissions and studies suggest that just one electric car on the road, could save an average of 1.5 million grams of CO_2 per year. This idea is further **evidenced** by countries such as Norway, where an increased uptake in the use of EVs has significantly reduced the country's level of carbon emissions.

3 Other advantages of EVs is that they perform well and don't require much **maintenance**. According to many car **manufacturers** EVs now outperform comparable diesel- or gasoline-powered cars. Furthermore, EVs are much quieter than **conventional** cars. Gasoline-fuelled cars are noisy due to the process of **combustion** occurring in each of the engine's cylinders. However, this is not necessary with EVs and therefore by comparison the driving experience can feel much smoother and quieter. Moreover, electric cars are more efficient to maintain. This is because the battery motor will not need oil changes, you will not need to replace engine parts, and generally EVs will not experience the same level of damage over time as a gasoline-fuelled car.

4 However, as with all new technologies, EVs do come with some notable **drawbacks**. One of the major difficulties with **banning** all fossil fuel cars is the cost implication. Although in the long term EVs might be cheaper to run, in the short term EVs are still quite expensive to buy. One of the main reasons for this is that the battery which powers the car is costly. It is the most expensive part of an EV because it is still relatively expensive to produce. However, as battery technologies improve, the price is predicted to decrease in the future.

5 Another significant disadvantage of EVs is that electric cars can travel less distance. The average range for an EV is estimated to be 340 km per charge, whereas some luxury models are able to reach 483 km plus per charge. However, these types of cars are expensive. For example, the Tesla Model X, which provides approximately 542 km of range, has a starting price of about £90,000. By comparison, the average gasoline or diesel vehicle can reach 483km on a full tank, and more fuel-efficient cars can achieve a much further distance. Fuelling an all-electric car can also be problematic. Fully recharging the battery pack can take up to eighty hours, and even fast charging stations can take 30 minutes to charge to 80% capacity. The location and availability of EV charging points is also a concern for those wanting to purchase an electric car. Although the EV charging infrastructure is expanding all the time, in many countries charging points are still not sufficiently accessible. Consequently, owners of EVs must plan their journeys carefully.

6 In conclusion, whilst owning an EV is clearly much better for the environment and will most probably become mandatory in the future, currently the initiative is still experiencing teething problems. However, once these technologies have been developed further, then EVs will have a very positive impact on societies worldwide.

[1]**on the brink of** (idiom) it is likely that a situation will happen soon
[2]**run on** (phr v) to use a particular supply of power
[3]**diesel** (n) a type of fuel
[4]**exhaust pipe** (n) the pipe at the back of the vehicle through which waste gas escapes from the engine

READING BETWEEN THE LINES

7 Work with a partner. Answer the questions based on the ideas in the essay.

1 Why must EV owners plan their journeys carefully?

2 Why does the writer say that EVs will have a positive impact in the future?

MAKING INFERENCES

DISCUSSION

8 Work with a partner. Use ideas from Reading 1 and Reading 2 to discuss the questions.

1 How can you limit the amount of energy you use per week with regards to travel / transport?

2 Does your country use a lot of renewable energy?

3 Do you think all cars will be electric in the future? Why / Why not?

SYNTHESIZING

WRITING

9 What could governments around the world do to encourage the use and purchase of electric cars? Write two paragraphs explaining your ideas.

⊙ LANGUAGE DEVELOPMENT

ENERGY COLLOCATIONS

1 In pairs look at the words in the triangle and try and create as many collocations as possible. Use a dictionary if needed.

Example: *alternative energy*

energy, fuel,

clean, air

renewable, nuclear,

source, diesel,

pollution, radioactive,

electricity, fossil, power

2 Complete the sentences using energy collocations from Exercise 1.

1 Nuclear _____ produces radioactive waste.
2 Traditionally cars have either been powered by petrol or _____ fuel.
3 We are running out of _____ fuels, such as oil and gas.
4 Rivers and lakes are two major _____ sources which can be used for hydroelectric power.

FORMAL AND INFORMAL ACADEMIC VERBS

3 Look at the informal piece of writing below and make it sound more formal by replacing the words in bold with the words from the box. Remember to change the verbs from the infinitive form to the appropriate tense.

> to manage   to instigate   to inform   to diminish
> to initiate   to utilize

There is no doubt that energy supplies are beginning **to run out** _____ *worldwide. The world's natural resources are being* **used** _____ *at an alarming rate – not only fossil fuels such as coal, oil and gas, but also water, wood, metals and minerals. This has many potential consequences for the billions of people who live on Earth. In recent years, both people and governments have become more interested in* **dealing with** _____ *the world's resources in a better way. While alternative energy solutions are important, they are not always practical. An immediate way to improve the situation is to encourage everyone to reduce, reuse and recycle.*
We must all learn to use fewer natural resources on a daily basis. We can **start** _____ *this by reducing the number of electrical items we leave plugged in or use less water. In our homes, we could use only energy-saving light bulbs and install water meters. Parents should* **tell** _____ *children from an early age to turn off lights which they are not using. Also, many cities are* **introducing** _____ *carbon emissions taxes, which is definitely a step in the right direction.*

4 Work with a partner. Answer the questions.

1 What do you think of the writer's ideas? Do you agree or disagree?
2 Can you think of any other ways we could conserve natural resources?

WRITING

CRITICAL THINKING

At the end of this unit, you will write an explanatory essay. Look at this unit's writing task below.

> Explain the advantages and disadvantages of three types of renewable energy and decide which would work best in your country.

1 Read the questions in the table. Look back at Reading 1 to help you complete the table. Give reasons for your ideas.

ANALYZE

	What are the benefits?	What are the drawbacks?	Is it effective for your country? What is the impact of producing it?
hydropower			
wind power			
solar energy			
biomass energy			
geothermal energy			

2 Compare your answers with a partner. Do his or her answers provide you with any extra information? If so, add this information to your table.

Evaluating benefits and drawbacks

When planning certain kinds of essays, you may be required to analyze specific benefits and drawbacks. Doing this can help you identify whether something is generally positive or negative, and for what reason. Collect the points you wish to make and organize them. Then, put them in order of importance, usefulness or interest.

SKILLS

3 Review your notes and decide on the three best options for your country from the energy sources below. Compare your answers with a partner.

EVALUATE

- hydropower
- wind
- solar
- biomass
- geothermal

4 Focus on your top three sources of energy. Write a sentence for each one that says why you think it would be a suitable alternative energy choice for your country. Use ideas from Reading 1 to help you.

Rank	Type of energy	Reason
1		
2		
3		

GRAMMAR FOR WRITING

RELATIVE CLAUSES

GRAMMAR

Relative clauses can define, describe or add extra information about nouns. In the example below, the part in bold is a relative clause.

Energy sources **which produce greenhouse gases*** *should not be used.*

The relative clause (*which produce greenhouse gases*) gives important information about the subject (*energy sources*).

*A relative clause must contain a subject and a verb, but it cannot be a sentence by itself.

Most relative clauses start with a relative pronoun (*who, which, that, whose*) or a relative adverb (*when, where*).

Use *who* or *that* for people.

Charles Fritts was the person **who/that first invented the solar panel in 1883**

Use *which* or *that* for things or ideas.

Tesla is the car manufacturer **which/that most people associate with electric cars**.

China is the country **where the most wind energy is currently generated**.

Use *when* for time.

The 1990s was the decade **when renewable energy sources increased in popularity**.

Use *whose* for possession.

A person **whose car runs on fossil fuels could be banned in the future**.

1 Underline the relative clause in each sentence and choose the correct relative pronoun. What subject does each relative clause refer to?

1 James Francis was the engineer *who / which* developed the first modern water turbine.

2 People *whose / where* houses are near renewable energy farms, can complain about the disruption to the area.

3 The cabinet *which / where* the electricity meter is located is locked.

4 It is sometimes cheaper to use electricity at night *which / when* fewer people are using it.

There are two kinds of relative clauses: *defining* and *non-defining*.

Defining relative clauses

Defining relative clauses give **essential information** about a noun.

*Wind turbines **which are offshore** are dangerous to marine mammals.*

As shown in the example, **in defining relative clauses commas are not needed**.

The defining relative clause here makes it clear **where** the wind turbines are.

If the clause is removed from the sentence, it would suggest that all wind turbines are dangerous to marine mammals, even the ones on land – so the information is 'essential'.

Non-defining relative clauses

Non defining relative clauses give extra, non-essential information about a noun.

*The solar panels, **which I had installed last year**, are working really well.*

The relative clause (*which I had installed last year*) is non-essential information.

If the clause is removed, the rest of the sentence still makes sense.

As shown in the example, **use commas before and after non-defining relative clauses.**

Do not use *that* in non-defining relative clauses. Use *who* for people and *which* for things.

*Elon Musk, **who owns Tesla**, is renowned for promoting the electric car.*
*Nuclear energy, **which is primarily generated by splitting atoms**, provides 11% of the world's energy supplies.*
✗ *Nuclear energy, **that is primarily generated by splitting atoms**, provides 11% of the world's energy.*

2 Complete the sentences with the correct relative pronoun. Add commas to the sentences with non-defining relative clauses.

1 Nuclear power stations _____ have poor safety records should be closed down.
2 Wind power _____ is a form of renewable energy is very popular in China.
3 There are certain solar panels _____ can produce almost a kilowatt of electricity per day.
4 Wind turbines _____ are located offshore are more expensive than wind turbines which are located on top of hills.
5 People _____ oppose renewable energy should consult facts.
6 Al Gore _____ is a key supporter of alternative energy won the Nobel Prize in 2007.

3 Read the text below and circle the correct relative pronouns.

While all countries face difficulties in the fight against pollution, China is [1] *which / where* the biggest challenge lies. With a population of 1.4 billion and a booming economy carbon emissions are high. Encouragingly however, it is also an economy [2] *which / who* is making significant progress in terms of green energy sources. Xi Jinping, [3] *which / who* is China's president, has pledged that China will reach carbon neutrality by 2060. China is currently the country [4] *which / where* produces the most solar power and the nation [5] *that / where* has triple the amount of wind installations compared to any other country.

ACADEMIC WRITING SKILLS

INTRODUCING ADVANTAGES AND DISADVANTAGES

You can use a range of phrases to introduce the advantages and disadvantages of ideas or solutions to problems.

*One **major** advantage of … is …*
*The **most obvious** benefits of … are …*
*One **other apparent** advantage of … is …*
*A **further possible** benefit of … is …*
*The **most serious** disadvantage of … is …*
*A **distinct** drawback of … is …*
*One **other inherent** disadvantage of … is …*
*Another **potential** drawback of … is …*

Notice how adjectives like *apparent*, *possible* and *potential* can be used to show less certain or less obvious advantages and disadvantages.

1 Complete the sentence below with one of the expressions from the box. There is more than one answer for each question.

1 _____ of geothermal energy is that the initial costs of installing the system are very high.

2 _____ of biomass is that it can re-grow over a relatively short period of time.

3 _____ of hydropower is that it can have a negative environmental impact on aquatic wildlife.

2 Imagine you live in a small village, and there is a plan to build a large solar farm near your home. Work with a partner and discuss the opposing views on this development. Use the ideas below to help you.

Person 1 (against the proposal): too big, rural landscape would change, harmful to wildlife, traffic chaos, impact on property values, etc.

Person 2 (for the proposal): help the environment, create jobs, etc.

COHERENCE

When writing, it is important to make the relationship between different ideas in a text clear to a reader. The ideas should flow in a logical way. This is called coherence, and it makes your writing easier for the reader to follow.

Some words you can use to make your writing coherent are:

1 **Pronouns** which refer back to an idea already introduced: *they, them, it, one,* etc.
   *There are many **types of renewable energy**. **They** are better for the environment than fossil fuels.*

2 **Determiners**: *this, that, these, those,* etc.
   *Solar power is a sustainable type of energy. **This** characteristic makes it attractive for those living in sunny places.*

3 **Conjunctions and connectors**: *however, therefore, in contrast, although,* etc.
   *Geothermal energy does not cause pollution. **However**, it is expensive to install.*
   *Reusing things is efficient and uses very little energy. **Therefore**, it is a viable alternative to recycling.*

4 **Transition words and phrases**: *for example, in the same way, still,* etc.
   *There are some dangers to hydropower. **For example**, the turbines might harm aquatic wildlife.*
   *It can be expensive or time-consuming to recycle rubbish. **Still**, the benefits are clear.*

3 Read the paragraph and complete the text with the words from the box below.

> for example   however   in the same way   they (×2)   this

People have different attitudes about alternative energy sources. (1)_____ , some people welcome the construction of wind turbines in their towns and cities. Others, (2)_____ , think that (3)_____ are undesirable. For (4)_____ second group of people, turbines are noisy and unattractive. (5)_____ that some people think hydropower dams are harmful to river environments, people who are against wind turbines think that (6)_____ ruin natural landscapes and pose dangers to local birds.

4 Read the sentences and write a coherent paragraph using all the information. Use Exercise 2 to help you.

1 Turbines and hydropower plants both change the landscape of an area.
2 Some think that they are important sources of alternative energy.
3 Fossil fuel use has been linked to global warming.
4 Some people are more concerned about using fossil fuels than other people are.
5 Some people think it is more important to save money than to reduce global warming.
6 Alternative energy production facilities can be expensive to construct.

_____
_____
_____
_____
_____
_____

WRITING TASK

Explain the advantages and disadvantages of three types of renewable energy and decide which would work best in your country. Write 350–400 words.

PLAN

1 Look back at Reading 1 and 2, which both examine the advantages and disadvantages of a topic. With a partner discuss how each article is structured and look the language used to write this type of essay.

2 Now look at the notes you wrote for the Critical Thinking section on page 137 and complete the plan below.

Introductory paragraph: (around 50 words) thesis statement	
Point 1 (energy type 1): (around 100 words) description advantage(s) disadvantage(s)	
Point 2 (energy type 2): (around 100 words) description advantage(s) disadvantage(s)	
Point 3 (energy type 3): (around 100 words) description advantage(s) disadvantage(s)	
Concluding paragraph: (around 50 words) a summary of your key points the preferred option for your country and why	

2 Refer to the Task checklist on page 144 as you prepare your essay.

ART AND DESIGN

LEARNING OBJECTIVES

Watch and listen
Watch and understand a video about an art district in Beijing.

Reading skill
Scan to find information.

Critical thinking
Understand and evaluate analogies.

Grammar
Paraphrase quotations; use substitution; use ellipsis.

Academic writing skill
Write arguments, counter-arguments and refutations.

Writing task
Write an argumentative essay.

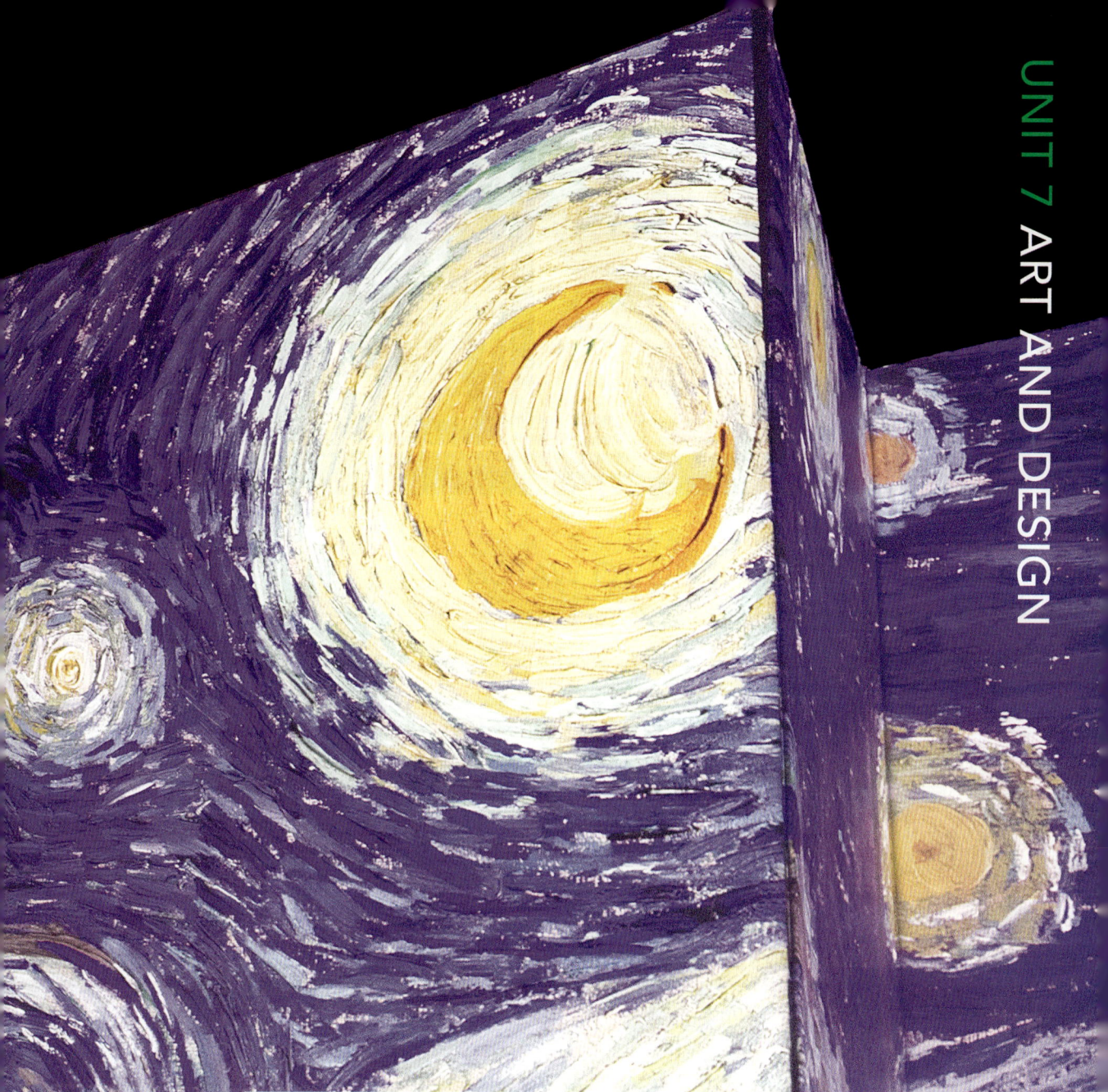

UNL**O**CK YOUR KNOWLEDGE

Work with a partner. Discuss the questions.

1 Look at the photo which shows somebody enjoying the Van Gogh immersive art experience. This is a three-dimensional experience of the artist's work. Do you think this type of exhibition is a good idea? Why / Why not?

2 What do you think art will look like in the future?

3 Do you like art and design? If so, what media (e.g. painting, music, architecture, fashion) do you like?

4 Is it important to study art and artists as a school subject? Why / Why not?

WATCH AND LISTEN

PREPARING TO WATCH

ACTIVATING YOUR KNOWLEDGE

1 Work with a partner and answer the questions.

1 Where can you find art, either in your own home city or town, or in a city you have visited?

2 Can you find art outside of museums? Where?

PREDICTING CONTENT USING VISUALS

2 Look at the pictures from the video. Discuss the questions with a partner.

1 Where do you think these pictures were taken?

2 How are these places different from where you usually find art?

3 Do you consider the pieces in the video art? Why / Why not?

GLOSSARY

state-run (adj) operated by the government

present a ... face (phr) give a ... impression

mainstream arts scene (phr) the places and ways in which well-known artists usually work and exhibit their work

struggling artist (n) an artist who works hard but whose work is not well known

WHILE WATCHING

UNDERSTANDING MAIN IDEAS

3 ▶ Watch the video. Which sentence best summarizes the main idea?

1 Art Zone 798 hosts art exhibitions, film festivals, fashion shows and theatre productions.

2 Art Zone 798 is a popular attraction today but soon another popular space will replace it.

3 Art Zone 798 began as a work space for struggling artists and is now a major arts centre.

4 ▶ **Watch again. Complete the summary.**

Years ago, Art Zone 798 was a (1)_____ . In the 1990s, after the buildings were abandoned, (2)_____ began to move in. It was the perfect space for the (3)_____ that many of these artists created. Many different kinds of artists worked at Art Zone 798, including (4)_____ , fashion designers, photographers and film directors. Soon, more well-known artists began to display their work there, and the centre became (5)_____ with tourists and local visitors. In addition to the art work, there are services for visitors, including (6)_____ . Struggling artists can no longer (7)_____ in Art Zone 798. They have moved to (8)_____ .

5 **Circle the statements you can infer from the video. Discuss your answers with a partner.**

1 The government opposed the centre when it began in the 1990s.
2 Some artists can earn a good income today in Beijing.
3 It may still be difficult for some artists to earn enough in Beijing.
4 There are many other centres like Art Zone 798 in Beijing.

DISCUSSION

6 **Discuss the questions with your partner.**

1 Would you like to visit Art Zone 798? Why / Why not?
2 Do you think there should be special spaces where struggling artists can work and show their work? Should the government support the space? Why / Why not?

READING 1

PREPARING TO READ

1 You are going to read a magazine article about the nature of art. Read the definitions. Complete the sentences with the words in bold.

> **aesthetic** (adj) relating to the enjoyment or study of beauty, or showing great beauty
> **conceptual** (adj) based on ideas or principles
> **contemporary** (adj) existing or happening now
> **distinction** (n) a difference between similar things
> **established** (adj) generally accepted or familiar; having a long history
> **notion** (n) a belief or idea
> **significance** (n) importance

1 A sculpture in which the artist's main idea or message is considered more important than the technique can be called _____ art.
2 The new museum in town has a lot of _____ appeal. The exterior of the building is very beautifully designed.
3 It is common these days to prefer _____ architecture, but I like the classic, old homes in my neighbourhood.
4 In art class we learned the _____ between fine art and applied art.
5 It is now well _____ that Pablo Picasso was one of the great artists of the twentieth century.
6 Art historians often explain the _____ of very famous works of art and how they may have influenced our society.
7 Many people share the _____ that the term 'art' also applies to things like car and video game design.

2 Read the descriptions (1–4) and match the artists to the photographs (a–d) of their work.

1 Andy Warhol: An artist who was famous for his colourful paintings of ordinary objects such as soup tins. _____

2 Damien Hirst: A radical British artist who famously used dead animals in his work. _____

3 Marcel Duchamp: An early twentieth-century French artist who changed what people thought of sculpture. _____

4 Yayoi Kusama: A Japanese artist famous for her use of bright colours and dots. _____

PREDICTING CONTENT USING VISUALS

WHILE READING

Scanning to find information

Scanning is a reading technique used to look for specific information in a text. If you know what information you want from a text, you do not need to read it all. Just move your eye quickly down the page looking for the key words related to the information you want. When you find the information, you can just read that part in detail.

SKILLS

3 Scan the magazine article on page 152 and put the artists in the order in which they are mentioned.

a Yayoi Kusama _____
b Damien Hirst _____
c Marcel Duchamp _____
d Andy Warhol _____

SCANNING TO FIND INFORMATION

ALL THAT ART IS

1 What is art? This question has puzzled philosophers and great thinkers for centuries. In fact, there is disagreement about exactly what art is. Most of us would agree that Leonardo da Vinci's *Mona Lisa* is art, but what about a video game? One dictionary definition states that art is 'making objects, images or music, etc. that are beautiful or that express certain feelings'. This, however, could be regarded as too broad a definition. There are actually a number of different categories of objects and processes under the umbrella term of art which can be explored.

2 Art is typically divided into two areas: fine art (such as painting, sculpture, music and poetry) and applied art (such as pottery, weaving, metalworking, furniture making and calligraphy). However, some claim that the art label can also be attached to car design, fashion, photography, cooking or even sports. Fine art is categorized as something which only has an **aesthetic** or **conceptual** function. This point was made over a thousand years ago by the Greek philosopher Aristotle, who wrote, 'The aim of art is to represent not the outward appearance of things but their inward **significance**'. He noted that artists produced objects, drama and music which reflected their emotions and ideas, rather than just trying to capture a true image of nature. Andy Warhol, the American artist famous for his Pop Art in the 1960s, once said, 'An artist produces things that people don't need to have'. This is the **distinction** between fine and applied art. Applied arts require an object to be functional as well as beautiful.

3 In the twentieth century, artists began to challenge the **established** idea of art. The French artist Marcel Duchamp changed people's **notion** of what sculpture was, for example, by mounting a bicycle wheel upside down on a stool in 1913 and calling it art. Duchamp said, 'Everything an artist produces is art'. In 2002, Japanese artist Yayoi Kusama created a viewer participation work called *The Obliteration Room*. In this work, a white room, with white furniture and objects, is covered by visitors with many colourful sticker dots. Today, many people complain about the lack of skill in the production of conceptual artistic objects. Some **contemporary** artists use assistants to produce all their art for them. British artist Damien Hirst claims that as long as he had the idea, it is his work. He has compared his art to architecture, saying, 'You have to look at it as if the artist is an architect, and we don't have a problem that great architects don't actually build the houses'.

4 Despite a hundred years of modern art, fine art is still regarded as a preserve of the wealthy. Hirst's works, for example, sell for millions of dollars. Even so, we can see examples of art all around us which are not expensive. Many towns and cities have public art which can be enjoyed by all. Some museums, like the National Art Museum of China in Beijing, are free. Others are free for children and students. Street art is also popular in different neighbourhoods around the world. One British artist, Banksy, has become world famous for unauthorized[1] works of art painted on building walls. These can be viewed at no charge by anyone who knows where to look for them.

5 Art anthropologist Ellen Dissanayake, in the book *What is Art For?*, offers one intriguing function of art: 'the heightening of existence'. In other words, art makes our ordinary, everyday lives a little more special. This notion may not apply to all art, but perhaps we can agree that it is a good goal towards which all artists should reach.

[1]**unauthorized** (adj) without official permission

Sweeping It Under the Carpet
by Banksy

4 Read the magazine article again. Write *T* (true), *F* (false) or *DNS* (does not say) next to the statements. Then correct the false statements.

_____ 1 The writer feels that the dictionary definition of art is too wide.

_____ 2 Metalworking is an example of fine art.

_____ 3 Some people argue that sports are a type of art.

_____ 4 Aristotle was the first to say that art should be affordable for all.

_____ 5 Andy Warhol invented Pop Art.

_____ 6 'Art for art's sake' refers to applied art.

_____ 7 Duchamp's bicycle wheel was sold at an art exhibition for a very high price.

_____ 8 Damien Hirst produces all his own art.

READING BETWEEN THE LINES

5 Which of the artists mentioned in the article would probably have these opinions? Write the names of the artists.

1 It is the idea of the work of art that is most important. _____

2 Art isn't functional. _____

3 Everything an artist makes can be considered art. _____

4 A building wall can be used like a canvas. _____

5 It does not matter if the artist doesn't actually make the work of art. _____

6 Everyone can be part of the creative process. _____

DISCUSSION

6 Work with a partner. Discuss the questions.

1 What do you think is the main purpose of art? Does it need to have a purpose, or can it just be beautiful?

2 Do you think video games should be classified as art? What about graffiti? Explain your answer.

WRITING

7 Choose one of the artists in Reading 1. Write a paragraph saying whether you agree or disagree with their view of what art is.

READING 2

PREPARING TO READ

USING YOUR KNOWLEDGE

1 You are going to read an essay about photography. Work in pairs and discuss the questions below.

1 Do you consider photography to be a form of art?
2 Do you like taking photographs? Why / Why not?

UNDERSTANDING KEY VOCABULARY

2 Read sentences (1–8) and try to understand the words in bold from the context. Then match them to their definitions (a–h).

1 Critics **perceived** him to be a great painter of real-life situations.
2 A camera is a **mechanical** device.
3 This artist uses different **mediums**, such as chalk, oil, paint, etc.
4 The artist uses a **sophisticated** 3D printer to create identical plastic models of real people. The models show great detail from the wrinkles in people's faces to the folds in their clothing.
5 News reporting, unlike other kinds of writing, is expected to be **objective** and not based on someone's opinion.
6 Although I do not think the artist had the right to paint on buildings without permission, I do **acknowledge** that his work is very imaginative.
7 I prefer sculptures that show something I can recognize rather than **abstract** ones.
8 The splash of white paint across the painting might look like an accident, but the artist placed it there **deliberately**.

a highly developed and complex
b not of real people or things
c materials used to create art
d based on facts and reality
e intentionally
f agree; admit something is true
g related to machines
h to think of someone or something in a particular way

WHILE READING

SCANNING TO FIND INFORMATION

3 Scan the essay opposite and answer the questions.

1 What does Ansel Adams say about photography?
2 According to Henri Cartier-Bresson what is the key to taking a successful photograph?
3 Why was Edward Steichen able to sell his photograph for a substantial amount of money?
4 According to the text, what other roles can photography have?

PHOTOGRAPHY AS ART

1 The production of fine art is the use of skill and imagination to create aesthetic objects or experiences which can be shared with other people. Photography is thought by some to be a form of fine art because it is made using the same critical and creative process that a painter or sculptor would use. It seems clear, however, that there is a significant difference between creating images by hand – using paint, clay or other tools – and pointing a **mechanical** device at something interesting and clicking. Although photography does have some features in common with other kinds of art, it cannot be said that photography is unquestionably art.

2 It is true that photography can be appreciated on the same level as other recognized forms of visual art. Sometimes decisions involved in creating a photograph are similar to those made by any other artist. A photograph is not always just a record of the world, but a **deliberately** created image with its own artistic features. Ansel Adams, the American photographer, commented on this point when he noted that *take* is not the right verb for a photograph. Instead, he said, one *makes* a photograph. To this end, there is a growing trend for photographers to call themselves artists. However, we cannot ignore the fact that artists can sell their pieces in the higher-priced, fine-art markets, whereas photographers usually cannot. A photograph by artist Edward Steichen, for example, recently sold for $11.8 million. No one would likely pay that much for a photograph unless the photographer presented himself as an artist.

3 Although some photography can be **abstract**, most photographs are basically **objective** records of a particular place at a particular time. Certainly we can appreciate a beautiful photograph when we see one, but any beauty that is **perceived** in the picture comes from the time and place where it was taken, and it is not the creation of the photographer. Also, **sophisticated** and expensive equipment often plays a greater role in the success of a photograph than the photographer's creativity. Even some of the greatest photographers **acknowledge** that there is a limit to the amount of influence they can have on a final product. Henri Cartier-Bresson, the famous French photographer, admitted that luck was the most important factor. Finally, photography is so widely used for practical functions that have little or nothing to do with art, such as police work, advertising and news reporting, that it cannot claim to be made for aesthetic purposes alone.

4 People have argued whether photography is art ever since the first photographers shared their work. A photographer may make the same aesthetic choices as a fine artist: subject matter, lighting, colour or even a theme or message. However, cameras can also be purely functional tools, capturing visual records and presenting information. Photography is a **medium** that can be used to make art, but that does not mean that all photography is art.

4 Read the essay again. Answer the questions.

1 Why does the writer say, 'it cannot be said that photography is unquestionably art'?

2 Does the writer believe that photography is or isn't art?

5 In pairs read through these statements in the text and try to paraphrase them in your own words.

Original statements

1 … any beauty that is perceived in the picture is the beauty of the time and place where it was taken, and it is not the creation of the photographer.

2 … there is a significant difference between creating images by hand – using paint, clay or other tools – and pointing a mechanical device at something interesting and clicking.

3 … photography is so widely used for practical functions that have little or nothing to do with art, such as police work, advertising and news reporting, that it cannot claim to be made for aesthetic purposes alone.

4 … he noted that *take* is not the right verb for a photograph. Instead, he said, one *makes* a photograph.

5 … no one would likely pay that much for a photograph unless the photographer presented himself as an artist.

Paraphrases

a *The value of a photograph comes from the natural world, not from the skill of the person holding the camera.*

b _____

c _____

d _____

e _____

6 Compare your paraphrases with another group. Are they similar?

7 Discuss in pairs. Do you agree or disagree with these statements? Give reasons for your answers.

8 Match the opinions (1–5) to the people (a–e).

Opinions

1 There's no reason for a great photograph to be any cheaper than a great painting. _____

2 Even a child could take a great picture of that view. _____

3 There's a lot more skill to making a picture than just pointing a camera at something and clicking. It's something that I create. _____

4 Most of us would just walk by and not notice something that could make a fabulous photo. And even if we did notice we probably wouldn't know how to take a photo that would stir other people's feelings. _____

5 Sometimes you just see something that will make a great picture and the light is perfect and you have your camera with you. At other times, nothing seems to be right. _____

People

a Ansel Adams

b Henri Cartier-Bresson

c Andreas Gursky

d The author of the essay

e Someone who believes photography is art

DISCUSSION

9 Work with a partner. Use ideas from Reading 1 and Reading 2 to discuss the following questions.

1 Do you think photographs should be worth as much as paintings?

2 Look at the statements in Exercise 6. Which one do you most strongly agree with? Think of an example to support your opinion.

3 In Reading 1, the artist Duchamp is quoted as saying, 'Everything an artist produces is art.' Do you agree or disagree with this idea?

◉ LANGUAGE DEVELOPMENT

PARAPHRASING QUOTATIONS

One very important skill in academic writing is **paraphrasing,** as shown in Exercise 5. Here are four techniques you can use to paraphrase:

1 **Use reported speech** – explaining someone else's opinion without using the same words by using reporting verbs such as a*dmit, state, say, feel, insist, believe, point out, emphasize, maintain, deny, suggest* and *theorize.*

'Of course, it's all luck.' – Henri Cartier-Bresson

Henri Cartier-Bresson, the famous French photographer, **admitted** *that luck was the most important factor.*

2 **Use synonyms or antonyms for key words.**

Henri Cartier-Bresson admitted that luck was a **significant component***.*

3 **Change the part of speech of some words.**

Henri Cartier-Bresson made an **admission** *that luck was important.*

4 **Change the sequence of the ideas in a sentence.**

Luck was important*, according to Henri Cartier-Bresson.*

Notice how all of these strategies are used in the paraphrase below.

Original quote: 'The chief enemy of creativity is good sense.' – Pablo Picasso

Paraphrase: *Pablo Picasso felt that doing things in the usual, sensible way was the main obstacle to imaginative art.*

1 Read the quotations and write sentences paraphrasing them. Your paraphrase should include the suggested language.

'A picture is worth a thousand words.' – Napoleon Bonaparte (use the verb *explain*)

Napoleon Bonaparte explained that a picture could tell us the same as a thousand words could.

1 'A picture is a poem without words.' – Horace (use the reporting verb *pointed out* and a synonym phrase for *poem*)

_____

2 'Creativity takes courage.' – Henri Matisse (use the reporting verb *felt* and an antonym for *courage*)

_____

3 'The painter has the universe in his mind and hands.' – Leonardo da Vinci (use the reporting verb *state* and sequence the ideas differently)

_____

2 Paraphrase the quotations using the strategies given opposite.

1 'Creativity is the power to connect the seemingly unconnected.' – William Plomer

_____

2 'I fight pain, anxiety and fear every day, and the only method I have found that relieves my illness is to keep creating art.' – Yayoi Kusama

_____

3 'Art enables us to find ourselves and lose ourselves at the same time.' – Thomas Merton

_____

3 In pairs discuss these quotes. Which ones do you agree or disagree with?

VOCABULARY FOR ART AND DESIGN

4 Match the adjectives in the box below to their definitions. Use a dictionary if needed.

> abstract   figurative   expressive   lifelike
> moving   avant-garde   powerful

1 it looks real: _____
2 having a strong effect on people: _____
3 involves shapes and colours and not images of real things or people: _____
4 a new and unusual style: _____
5 showing your feelings: _____
6 causing strong feelings of sadness and sympathy: _____
7 shows people, places, or things in a similar way to how they look in real life: _____

5 In pairs, use the adjectives from Exercise 4 to describe the pictures below.

GRAMMAR FOR WRITING

SUBSTITUTION

In academic writing, writers try to avoid repetition when possible. To do this, you can substitute pronouns or other words for nouns or noun phrases. In the sentence below, this is used to avoid repetition.

*Although many people find cars beautiful, ~~finding cars beautiful~~ **this** does not make cars art.*
Here, two pronouns are used in this way:

A work of art can mean different things to different people.
***That** is one reason people may find **it** interesting.*

1 Read the paragraph below about the fashion designer Issey Miyake. Underline the words used in order to avoid repeating his name.

Issey Miyake was a Japanese fashion designer who was born in 1938 in Hiroshima, and he died in 2022. Even early on in his career, this inspirational figure was very expressive with his style and he didn't conform to traditional ideas of what fashion should be. His catwalk shows were like art exhibitions and they often evoked a reaction from the public. Between 1996 and 1999, the innovator collaborated with artists as part of his Guest Artist series. Miyake stated that his intention was not to answer the question 'Is fashion art?' but instead to create a relationship between art and the people who admired it. By wearing the visionary's clothes people were experiencing art and fashion at the same time.

ELLIPSIS

Another way to avoid repetition is to leave out some words which have already been mentioned. This is called ellipsis.

*Some photos have a very clear meaning, but other photos **do not** ~~have a clear meaning~~.*

2 Read the paragraph and cross out any words or phrases which can be removed without affecting the meaning of the text. Add any substitutions (such as pronouns) which you think are necessary.

Many chefs regard themselves as artists and they see cooking very much as a creative process when they are making a dish. Several Michelin star chefs have defended this claim by stating that their food can cause people to have an emotional reaction, just as art can cause people to have an emotional reaction. Further to this, they say that a dish is prepared just like a painting, and they get their inspiration from the world around them, as is the case with great works of art. For these Michelin star chefs preparing food isn't just about feeding people's appetites, it is a passion and an expression of their artistry, just as an artist would do.

ACADEMIC WRITING SKILLS

ARGUMENTS – USING FACTS, STATISTICS AND LOGIC TO STENGTHEN YOUR ARGUMENT

Arguments

In academic writing, it is important to know how to create **an effective argument**. Using **facts, statistics** or **other kinds of examples** will make your argument more convincing. Also, **the logic** of your **argument should be clear.**

Here is an example of a weak argument:

This painting is not good because I don't like it.

This argument is weak because it does not contain any evidence and only gives the writer's opinion.

Here is an example of a stronger argument:

This painting is not good because it does not evoke any emotion for me, and I find the subject matter dull. For example, the painting next to it is a much livelier piece and I really feel a connection to the theme of the painting.

This argument is much stronger because the writer has added an example and logic to their argument.

1 Read each pair of arguments and circle the stronger argument. Explain why you think the other argument is weaker.

1
a Video games have visual effects, so I think they can be considered as art.
b Some video games can cause a great emotional response from the player, and this is at the root of all art forms.

_____

2
a Fashion is art because fashion designers have to make decisions about colour.
b Fashion design is an art form because it has influenced culture and different trends over time.

_____

3
a Students should study art because, in my opinion, it is fun to create art.
b Students should study art because it has been linked with general success in other subject areas.

_____

Counter-arguments and refutations

You can strengthen your argument by giving a *counter-argument* and a *refutation*. By presenting the counter-argument, you show that you have considered another point of view. By refuting it with reasons and evidence, you show why the counter-argument does not weaken your own point of view.

Consider this argument:

Photography is a useful medium, but it is not art.

The writer follows this with a counter-argument:

It is true that photography and fine art have some things in common.

Then the writer gives a refutation. Refuting the counter-argument shows the strength of the writer's position:

However, it is still the case that using your hands to create art requires more imagination than using a mechanical device.

The phrase 'However, it is still the case that …' indicates the author's argument is still valid.

2 Work with a partner. Complete these counter-argument and refutation sentences in a way which makes sense.

1 Critics of mandatory art education say that art is not as important as academic subjects. Even though that might be true,

_____ .

2 Some people believe that art is only for the rich. However,

_____ .

3 Opponents of public funding for art

_____ .

Nevertheless, public art beautifies our town and enriches our community culture.

3 Read the arguments and counter-arguments and give a refutation.

1 **Argument:** Making music is art, just like paintings and sculptures.
Counter-argument: Music is not art because it cannot be seen.
Refutation: _____

2 **Argument:** Graffiti artists deserve praise and recognition for their work.
Counter-argument: Many critics do not believe that graffiti artists like Banksy should receive praise for their work because it is illegal.
Refutation: _____

4 Work in pairs. Compare your answers and refutations. Do you agree? If not, explain to your partner why you think you are right.

WRITING TASK

Fashion, cooking and video games have all been likened to fine art. Choose one of these and discuss whether it should be considered fine art, comparable to painting or sculpture. Write 350–400 words

PLAN

1 Look back at your notes in Critical thinking. Create an outline for your essay using the following structure.

Introduction (50–100 words) Give a brief introduction to your chosen topic + thesis statement / your opinion
Body Paragraph 1 (100 words) Argument 1 (supported by counter-arguments / refutations or facts, statistics and examples)
Body Paragraph 2 (100 words) Argument 2 (supported by counter-arguments / refutations or facts, statistics and examples)
Conclusion (50–100 words) summarise the key points in your essay and re-instate your opinion

2 Refer to the Task checklist below as you prepare your essay.

WRITE A FIRST DRAFT

3 Write your essay.

REVISE

4 Use the Task checklist to review your essay for content and structure.

TASK CHECKLIST	✔
Did you provide strong arguments for your position, supported by some examples of logic, facts or statistics?	
Did you provide some counter-arguments and refutations?	
Did you paraphrase information correctly?	

5 Make any necessary changes to your essay.

EDIT

6 Use the Language checklist to edit your essay for language errors.

7 Make any necessary changes to your essay.

OBJECTIVES REVIEW

1 Check your learning objectives for this unit. Write *3*, *2* or *1* for each objective.

3 = very well   2 = well   1 = not so well

I can ...

watch and understand a video about an art district in Beijing. _____

scan to find information. _____

understand and evaluate analogies. _____

paraphrase quotations. _____

use substitution. _____

use ellipsis. _____

write arguments, counter-arguments and refutations. _____

write an argumentative essay. _____

2 Use the *Unlock* Digital Workbook for more practice with this unit's learning objectives.

UNLOCK
DIGITAL
WORKBOOK

WORDLIST

abstract (adj)	distinction (n) ◉	moving (adj)
acknowledge (v) ◉	established (adj)	notion (n) ◉
aesthetic (adj)	expressive (adj)	objective (adj)
avant-garde (adj) ◉	figurative (adj)	perceive (v) ◉
conceptual (adj)	lifelike (adj)	significance (n) ◉
contemporary (adj)	mechanical (adj)	sophisticated (adj)
deliberately (adv)	medium (n) ◉	

◉ = high-frequency words in the Cambridge Academic Corpus

AGEING

LEARNING OBJECTIVES

Watch and listen
Watch and understand a video about growing old.

Reading skill
Identify evidence in a text.

Critical thinking
Draw appropriate conclusions from graphical data.

Grammar
Use verb phrases to show cause and effect; use language of prediction; use the first conditional.

Academic writing skill
Use numerical words and phrases; interpret graphs and charts.

Writing task
Write an analysis essay.

UNL⌀CK YOUR KNOWLEDGE

Work with a partner. Discuss the questions below.

1 Look at the photo showing a grandfather and his grandson. What can the younger generation can learn from the older generation?

2 What do you think the secret is to living a long and healthy life?

3 When do you think old age starts? What do you think it will be like?

4 How is respect shown to elderly people in your culture?

WATCH AND LISTEN

PREPARING TO WATCH

ACTIVATING YOUR KNOWLEDGE

1 Work with a partner and answer the questions.

  1 Consider the three stages of life below:

    childhood (0–18)   adulthood (18–65)   old age (65 +)

    Which do you think is the best stage of life and why?

  2 What do you think are the benefits and drawbacks of each of these stages?

  3 Do you think people should fear getting older? Why / Why not?

PREDICTING CONTENT USING VISUALS

2 Look at the photos from the video. Discuss the questions with a partner.

  1 What are the people doing in each of these photos?

  2 What benefits might these activities provide?

  3 Looking at the photos, what do you predict the video will say about old age?

GLOSSARY

myth (n) an idea that is not true but is believed by many people

unachievable (adj) something that is impossible to achieve

impulsive (adj) showing behaviour in which you do things suddenly without any planning

immune system (n) the cells and tissues in the body that make it able to protect itself against infection

allergy (n) a condition that makes people become sick or develop skin or breathing problems because they have eaten certain foods or been near certain substances.

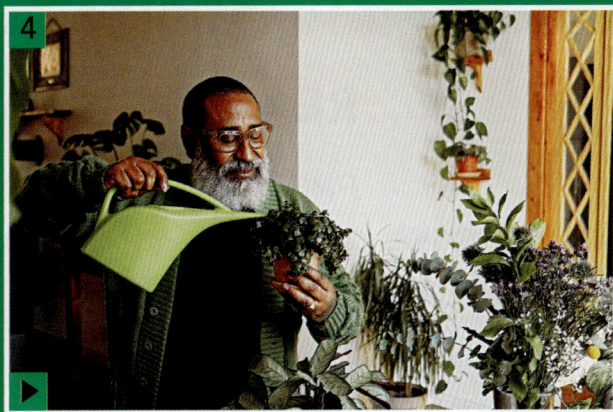

WHILE WATCHING

UNDERSTANDING MAIN IDEAS

3 ▶ **Watch the video. Which statement summarizes the main idea?**

1 People are happier in old age because they are less ambitious and more accepting of the life they have.
2 Youth is the most enjoyable stage, but old age can be rewarding.
3 People are happiest in old age and have more free time, but poverty and loneliness may be problems.
4 We should not fear ageing, as it can be an enjoyable stage in life. However, we must continue to exercise and try new hobbies.

UNDERSTANDING DETAIL

4 ▶ **Watch again. For each main idea, write a supporting detail.**

1 When we are older, our relationships improve.
_____

2 As we age, we forget unachievable ambitions.
_____

3 Age also gives us new skills.
_____

4 Our bodies and our brains improve, too.
_____

MAKING INFERENCES

5 Work with a partner. Discuss the questions.

1 Why do you think the study found that people were happiest in their sixties and seventies (after retirement)?
2 Why do think people in their twenties and thirties might focus on climbing the career ladder?

DISCUSSION

6 Work with a partner. Describe an elderly person you know and admire.

READING

READING 1

PREPARING TO READ

UNDERSTANDING
KEY VOCABULARY

1 Read the sentences (1–6) and write the words in bold next to the definitions (a–f).

1 Social scientists use **demographic** information to understand more about the populations of cities.

2 It is sometimes more difficult for older people to **adapt** to fast-changing technology than it is for younger people.

3 You should ask someone else for help because I don't have time to **undertake** a new project right now.

4 In her **capacity** as head of the hospital, she makes many decisions about the budget and the staff.

5 At my school, some activities are required for all students, but others are **voluntary**.

6 In my **leisure** time, I enjoy working in my garden.

a _____ (n) a particular position or job; a role

b _____ (adj) relating to human populations and information such as their size, growth, ages and education

c _____ (n) the time away from work and other duties

d _____ (adj) done without being forced or paid to do it

e _____ (v) to adjust to different conditions or uses

f _____ (v) to take responsibility for and begin doing something

USING YOUR
KNOWLEDGE

2 You are going to read an interview about ageing. Use your knowledge to write three facts which might be in the interview.

1 _____

2 _____

3 _____

3 Try to predict the answers to the questions.

1 To what extent has healthcare improved over the last 50 years?

2 Have these improvements been universal, or only in certain countries?

3 What kinds of problems might old people face in today's society?

4 What kinds of problems might a society face if it has more elderly people?

5 What kinds of benefits can an older population bring to society?

WHILE READING

4 Read the interview to check your ideas. If your ideas were different, why do you think that is?

THE SOCIAL AND ECONOMIC IMPACT OF AGEING

In the next instalment of our series on **demographic** changes, we interview Professor Robert Huffenheimer, an expert on the phenomenon of ageing.

1 What exactly does ageing mean?

It means the population in many countries is, on average, getting older. According to a United Nations report, in 2050, there will be more people over the age of 60 than children under 16 for the first time in history.

2 What impact is this ageing process likely to have globally?

Well, obviously it is a good thing that people are living longer, but as a result of this, there are a number of issues which have to be dealt with.

3 For example?

In certain countries, an increasing number of older people are living by themselves, often without any relatives living nearby. The UN reports that 40% of the world's older population lives independently. Some older people are simply unable to take care of themselves, and others can only do so if their houses are specially **adapted**. Likewise, they may be unable to go shopping or wash themselves. Consequently, they need someone, perhaps a professional, to help. And, of course, older people need social activities as well.

4 And how are societies adapting to this?

Supermarkets, for example, have introduced more home-delivery services, which have been particularly beneficial for older people. In addition, there has been significant growth in companies providing services which would traditionally have been **undertaken** by relatives. These include private nursing care and 'Meals on Wheels' services, which deliver food to your door. In the USA, for example, Meals on Wheels serves nearly 2.2 million elderly people across the country, many of whom are living alone or isolated, according to the Urban Institute.

5 Are there any other areas where the impact of ageing can be clearly seen?

Although it is not a problem yet, many governments are worried about the economic impact of an ageing population. Fewer citizens working and paying taxes obviously results in less money for the government to pay for things like health and education. NBC World News recently reported that in Italy, which has Europe's oldest population, people are now living 30 to 40 years beyond retirement. This means that the number of needy pensioners[1] is rising.

6 What advantages can an older population bring?

Countries with a high percentage of young people need to spend a lot of money on education. In contrast, countries with a lower percentage of children have fewer education costs. In more developed countries, older people tend to have more savings and more **leisure** time. In Japan, for example, according to Bloomberg News, the popularity of luxury train travel among older Japanese people has exploded. Consequently, luxury routes are often sold out. Other elderly people may spend more time online or even go back to studying. Of course, older people do have a lot of experience, and if they can, some continue working in a **voluntary capacity** after they retire[2]. This kind of activity adds a lot to society.

[1]**pensioner** (n) a retired person who receives government money for living expenses
[2]**retire** (v) to leave your job or stop working because of having reached a particular age

5 Read the interview again. Write *T* (true), *F* (false) or *DNS* (does not say) next to the statements. Correct the false statements.

_____ 1 Robert Huffenheimer teaches at Columbia University.

_____ 2 The average age of the world's population has increased significantly over the last 50 years.

_____ 3 Most older people have relatives nearby.

_____ 4 There are both benefits and disadvantages for societies with ageing populations.

_____ 5 So far, most private companies have ignored the changing demographic situation.

_____ 6 Most countries with an older population have much higher education costs.

_____ 7 On average, older people spend four hours per day online.

_____ 8 Countries can benefit from the skills of retired people.

6 Complete the sentences using words from the interview.

1 Specially adapted houses help elderly people who can't _____ _____ themselves.

2 Older people require _____ _____ as well as professional help with shopping and washing.

3 Home deliveries and _____ _____ _____ are commercial services provided for the elderly.

4 Governments are concerned about the _____ _____ of a large number of elderly people in the population who are not working.

5 Older people are free to travel and learn new skills because they have more _____ and _____ .

6 Experienced older people may choose to do work on a _____ basis to help society.

READING BETWEEN THE LINES

Identifying evidence in a text

Writers need to use persuasive language when making an argument, but it is even more important that good evidence is presented. Writers need to be able to justify everything they say. For example, the evidence presented about Italy in the text is supported by statistics from a news source. When you read claims in a text, look for evidence that the writer uses to justify his or her claim.

7 Work with a partner. Discuss the following questions.

1 Professor Robert Huffenheimer cites NBC World News to present two pieces of evidence to support his point. Can you identify them?
2 Huffenheimer cites Bloomberg News to mention the increase in luxury train travel in Japan. What effect does that citation have in the interview?
3 NBC World News and Bloomberg News are both internationally well-known news sources. How might this affect the persuasiveness of using them for support?

DISCUSSION

8 Work with a partner. Discuss the questions.

1 What problems do elderly people in your community face?
2 What does your local community do to help elderly people socially? What more could be done?
3 What do you think can be done to ensure that elderly people in society are protected and cared for?

READING 2

PREPARING TO READ

1 Work with a partner. Discuss the following questions.

USING YOUR KNOWLEDGE

1 Do you know of any countries with a greater percentage of young people?
2 Do you think having a young population has more advantages than having an ageing population? Why / Why not?

2 You are going to read an essay about the effects of a young population on a society. Work with a partner. Read the quiz questions and try to understand the words in bold from context. Use a dictionary to help you.

1 When was life expectancy first **documented**?
   a 1660s   b 1890s   c 1730s

2 What is the current **median** age of people in the UK?
   a 30   b 40   c 22

3 What **proportion** of people in Japan are 65 and over?
   a around 40%   b around 10 %   c around 30 %

4 According to the UN, what age **range** is considered to be elderly?
   a 70+   b 60+   c 80+

5 According to Dan Buetnner, an expert in living longer, what is the best way to **cope** with old age?
   a Move often and wake up with a sense of purpose
   b Get plenty of rest
   c Become a vegetarian

6 Which country has the lowest **pension** age in the world?
   a Japan   b China   c France

WHILE READING

3 Read the essay. What are the advantages and disadvantages of Saudi Arabia having a younger population?

What are the impacts of a young population on a society?

1 There is a well-**documented** problem with the ageing of the global population, but there are also areas of the world where the demographics are very different. In many parts of the Middle East and North Africa, there is a much higher **proportion** of young people. The Kingdom of Saudi Arabia, a country of over 35 million people, is one such place. This reality has brought special challenges to the Kingdom in a number of different areas such as education, housing and the economy.

2 The population graph shows the population of men and women in Saudi Arabia and their age **ranges** in 2023. The graph shows Saudi Arabia has a very young population. Upon close analysis, it can be seen that about 24% of the population is aged 14 and under, and approximately 13% of the total population is between the ages of 15 and 24. The number of Saudis in their mid-twenties to mid-fifties is particularly high, with almost 52% of the total population falling within this age range. In the United States the **median** age is 38, in the United Kingdom it is 40, in Italy it is 47 and in Japan it is 49. In contrast, Saudi Arabia is more youthful, as the median age is 30.5.

3 The high percentage of children and young people leads to high education costs in Saudi Arabia. The focus on education is a high priority for Saudi society. A recent report showed that education receives 17% of the government's annual budget, making the country's education spending one of the highest in the world. As a result of its demographic profile, the government has been leading a university expansion programme to **cope** with the large number of college-aged students moving through the school system every year.

4 This also has an impact on employment opportunities for young people. Youth unemployment could well become the Kingdom's biggest social challenge in the coming years. These days, the unemployment rate for Saudis between the ages of 15 and 24 is 33% Unless Saudi Arabia's government can provide enough public-sector jobs, or attract more private-sector employers, more budget expenditure will be needed for unemployment benefits.

5 There is a similar challenge in terms of housing, with more demand than supply. This is a particular problem in places such as Jeddah, Saudi Arabia's second-largest city. Jeddah is on the coast, with a mountain range to the east. Because of this, outward expansion is geographically impossible. As a consequence, houses have become more expensive, and young people may be unable to buy their own homes.

6 Although Saudi Arabia faces several challenges in terms of education, employment and housing as a result of its young population, it does not have to cope with the demands of an ageing population. Because the country has relatively fewer old people than the places mentioned earlier, the costs of healthcare and **pensions** are lower. This will allow more funds to be allocated to improving the lives of young people.

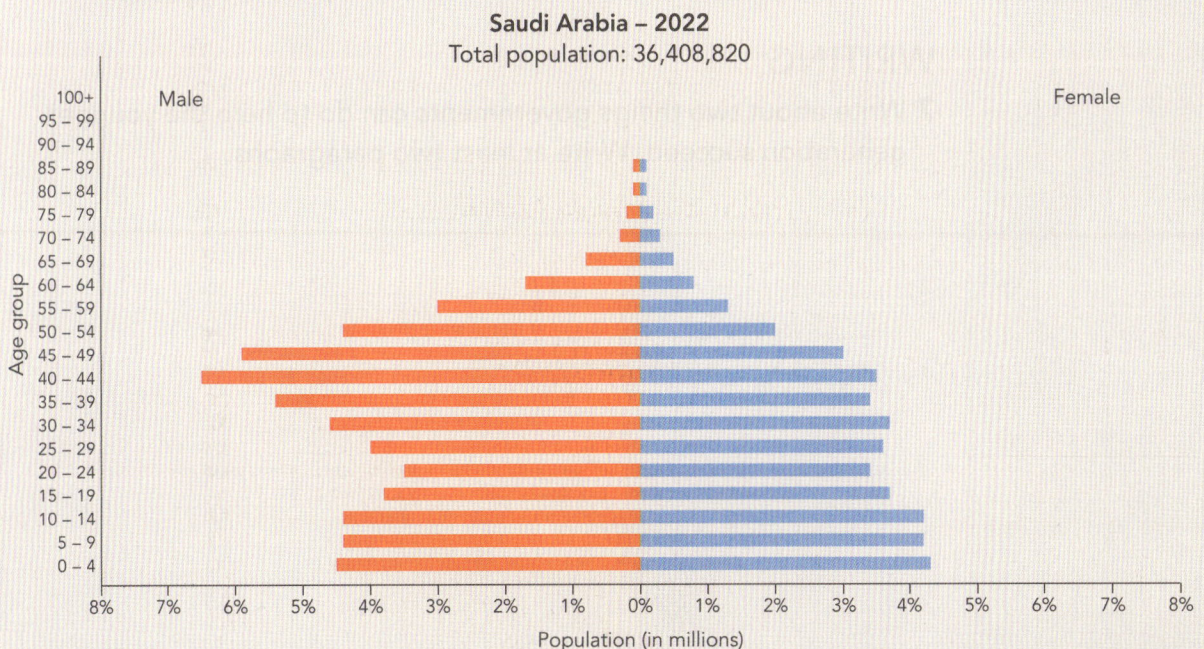

Saudi Arabia – 2022
Total population: 36,408,820

Population pyramid chart showing Male (left) and Female (right) populations by age group, with age groups from 0–4 up to 100+ on the vertical axis, and Population (in millions) on the horizontal axis ranging from 8% to 0% (Male side) and 0% to 8% (Female side).

4 Read the essay again. Answer the questions below:

  1 How much of the population in Saudi Arabia is aged between 25 to 55?

  2 How much does the Saudi government invest in education each year?

  3 What is the median age in Italy?

  4 What percentage of young people aged 15–24 do not have a job in Saudi Arabia?

READING BETWEEN THE LINES

5 Work with a partner. Find these words and phrases in the essay and discuss what they mean.

  1 demographics

  2 proportion

  3 sector

  4 expenditure

  5 allocated

  6 funds

DISCUSSION

6 Work with a partner. Use ideas from Reading 1 and Reading 2 to discuss the questions.

  1 What do you think is the best age to be? Why?

  2 Is there any help in your country for the younger generation to secure employment?

  3 Is there any help in your country for the younger generation to buy a property?

WRITING

7 Write about two things governments can do to help the younger generation succeed. Write at least two paragraphs.

⦿ LANGUAGE DEVELOPMENT

ACADEMIC COLLOCATIONS WITH PREPOSITIONS

1 Make collocations using one word from Box A, and one word from Box B.

A

| range   contract   rely   theory   sum   focus   brief |

B

| in   on   with   up   of |

rely on

2 Complete the sentences with the correct phrases and phrasal verbs from Exercise 1.

1 In your culture, who do the older generation _____ for help and support?

2 Is there a wide _____ opportunities for retired people to socialise and feel part of a community in your areas?

3 Do you think your country _____ the problems faced by the elderly, more than their valuable contribution to society?

4 The younger generation face the challenge of finding housing and employment, whereas _____, the older generation often need to tackle issues such as heartcare and loneliness. In your country, which sector of society needs the most help? Give reasons for your answer.

5 Is there a _____ activities available for the younger generation to participate in, in your local community? If so, what are they?

6 What areas of work do you think the younger generation need to _____ in order to be successful in the future?

3 In pairs, discuss the questions in Exercise 2.

CAUSE AND EFFECT

There are simple verb phrases we can use to show the cause and effect of certain actions.

*Ageing **results in** greater life experience and wisdom.*

*Ageing **leads to** greater life experience and wisdom.*

We can also use more complex linkers to show the connection between two sentences.

*Retired people in developed countries have more leisure time. **As a result of this / Subsequently**, they can travel more or even go back to studying.*

*Retired people in developed countries have more leisure time. **Because of this**, they can travel more or even go back to studying.*

*Retired people in developed countries have more leisure time. **As a consequence / Consequently**, they can travel more or even go back to studying*

4 Read the cause-and-effect example below:

Cause: *Many older people now live alone.*
Effect: *Some are lonely.*
Sentence: *Many older people now live alone; consequently some are lonely.*

5 Complete the following and try to use a variety of linkers in your sentences.

1 Cause: *In a country with a young population, securing a job could be challenging.*
Effect: _____
_____

Sentence: _____
_____

2 Cause: *Most people cannot afford private care in old age.*
Effect: _____
_____

Sentence: _____
_____

3 Cause: *It can be challenging for the younger generation to buy a property.*
Effect: _____
_____

Sentence: _____
_____

Compare your answers with a partner. Did you have similar ideas?

6 In pairs, discuss possible solutions to these four issues.

CRITICAL THINKING

At the end of this unit, you will write an analysis essay. Look at this unit's writing task below.

> Describe population trends in Japan. Use the data from the bar chart as evidence to support your claims. Suggest the potential impact on the country if the 2050 projections are correct. Write 350–400 words

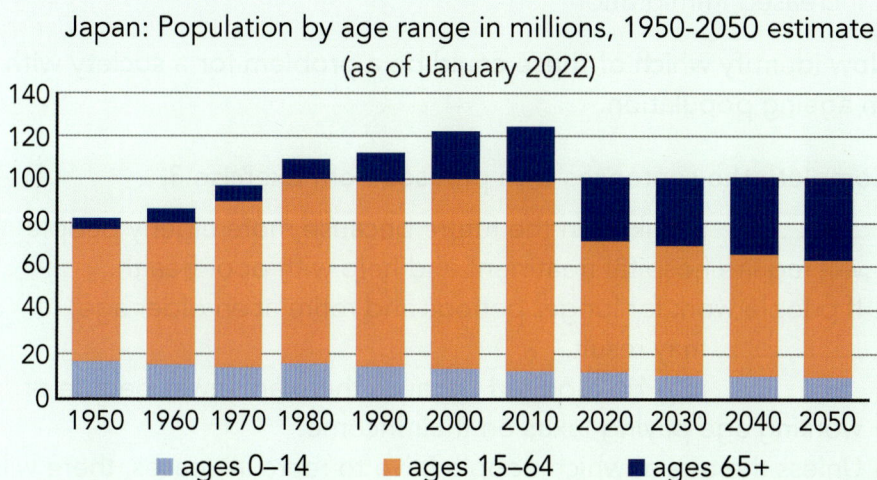

Japan: Population by age range in millions, 1950-2050 estimate (as of January 2022)

■ ages 0–14   ■ ages 15–64   ■ ages 65+

Source: *Japan Statistical Yearbook*

Drawing appropriate conclusions from graphical data

When writing about data, whether in the form of tables, graphs or diagrams, it is important to analyze it carefully, before drawing accurate conclusions. Look for the key messages which the data show, and don't focus on irrelevant information.

SKILLS

1 Look back at the graph of Saudi Arabia's population in Reading 2 on page 177. Answer the following questions.

ANALYZE

   1 When was the data in the graph recorded?
   2 What is the total population of Saudi Arabia?
   3 Are there more people over or under 65 in Saudi Arabia?
   4 Does Saudi Arabia have more men or more women?

2 Look at the population chart for Japan and answer the questions.

   1 When was the graph created?
   2 What is the approximate total population of Japan now?
   3 Are there more people over 65 or under 15 in Japan?
   4 How is the graph different from the one for Saudi Arabia in Reading 2? What are the reasons for this?

3 Work with a partner. Discuss what the following terms mean.

1 youth unemployment
2 housing shortages
3 higher pension costs
4 increased healthcare costs
5 stress on the education system
6 lower consumer spending
7 declining birth rate
8 higher taxes
9 increased emigration
10 increased immigration

4 Now identify which of these could be a problem for a society with an ageing population.

5 Complete the sentences with phrases from Exercise 3.

1 _____ are likely in the future because more elderly people will require hospital treatment and help with poor health.
2 If people work for longer periods and retire at an older age, _____ may result.
3 _____ may be required because there are fewer people of working age paying taxes on their income.
4 Unless the age at which people have to retire increases, there will be _____ which taxes will need to pay for.
5 As the population ages, there are fewer people having children. This _____ means that the population will actually decrease.
6 In order to replace the lost workforce and to increase levels of taxation, _____ may be encouraged by government policies.

6 Work with a partner. Look at the statements. Which advantage of an older population do you think is the most important? Why?

1 Older people have a great deal of knowledge and experience, which are valuable in the workplace.
2 Older people have more time and money to help their children and grandchildren financially or through helping with childcare and household chores.
3 Older societies result in a slower global population growth.
4 Older people these days are active and productive. Many have savings to help pay for their own healthcare and a comfortable standard of living.

GRAMMAR FOR WRITING

LANGUAGE OF PREDICTION

When you describe a graph, you can sometimes predict what might happen in the future based on the trends in the graph. You can use a number of different ways to show that a statement is a prediction.

Introduce a strong prediction: … *be likely to*, … *be set to*, … *be predicted to*, … *be expected to*, … *be projected to*

The younger generation **are expected to be** *more digitally literate than this generation.*

Introduce a weak prediction: … *may be*

Young people **may be** *unable to buy their own homes.*

Introduce a strong negative prediction: … *be unlikely to*

The population is **unlikely** *to get any younger.*

1 Make predictions about the next ten years using the language in the box above.

   1 Employment: *In the next* **ten** *years* **the job market is set to change considerably for the younger generation.**

   2 Care for the elderly: _____
_____

   3 Opportunities for the younger generation: _____
_____

   4 The housing market: _____
_____

   5 Education: _____
_____

2 Discuss your predictions with a partner. Are your predictions similar?

3 Make four predictions about your partner using the language from the box. Use the prompts below to help you.

   1 travel e.g. *I think you are likely to travel to Europe to visit your relatives.*

   2 jobs

   3 family

   4 study

THE FIRST CONDITIONAL

The **first conditional** describes possible situations in the future **that are likely to happen**, using an *if*-clause.

*Governments **will need to** address increasing pension costs **if the median age continues** to rise.*

Use the **future verb form** in the main clause and the **present simple** in the *if*-clause.

Use a comma after the *if*-clause only when it begins the sentence.

*If the median age continues to rise, governments **will need to** address increasing pension costs.*

In formal writing, you can use more complex linkers to replace *if*, such as **provided that**, **as long as** and **on the condition that**.

Provided that your unemployment benefits claim is approved, you will receive your first payment within two weeks.

*You will receive your first payment within two weeks **provided that** your unemployment benefits claim is approved.*

4 Circle the best verb forms to complete each sentence.

1 A country *faces / will face* problems in the future if the population *ages / will age* too much.

2 As long as medical technology *continues / will continue* to improve, people *live / will live* longer than before.

3 Once my father stops being able to live independently, I *move in / will move in* with him on the condition that he *agrees / will agree*.

4 If Saudi Arabia *does not create / will not create* programmes for the unemployed youth, *it faces / will face* a big social challenge.

5 Complete the following sentences and add a comma where necessary.

1 Provided that I have enough money I will travel to _____ .

2 As long as I am healthy in old age I will _____ .

3 _____ if I am given the opportunity in my work/studies.

4 With regards to hobbies _____ provided that I have the time.

ACADEMIC WRITING SKILLS

NUMERICAL WORDS AND PHRASES

> It is important to simplify complex statistical information when writing a description of a graph or chart. To do this, you can use generalizations to introduce the data and specific examples to give details or justify a claim. Numerical words and phrases help you do this.

1 Look at the pie chart about the population of Japan and complete the sentences with words from the box.

Population by age

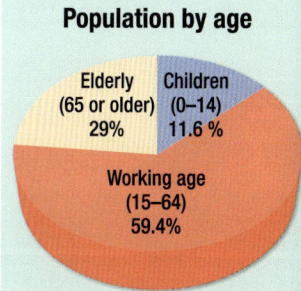

Elderly (65 or older) 29%
Children (0–14) 11.6%
Working age (15–64) 59.4%

> double   half   majority   minority   proportion
> quarter   times   triple

1 The overwhelming _____ of Japanese people are of working age.
2 A sizeable _____ (about 29%) are over 65 years old.
3 The number of Japanese people who are of working age is almost five _____ more than those under 14.
4 A significant _____ of the Japanese population is of working age.
5 The percentage of people aged 65 and older is nearly _____ the percentage of children.
6 The percentage of the population who are of working age is nearly _____ that of the elderly.
7 More than _____ the population is of working age.
8 Just under a _____ of the population is over 65.

INTERPRETING GRAPHS AND CHARTS

> When you write an analysis of information presented on a graph or a chart, keep in mind the following guidelines:
> - You **should introduce the chart** and say what it is about.
> - You **do not need to explain all of the data** shown, **just the important trends**
> - You **should use accurate figures** for the data that you refer to.
> - You should **analyse the data and make predictions** (if it is possible to do so).
> - **Do not include comments** which **are not related to the main points**.

The diagram below shows the global population by age in 1950 and 2000, and projected population figures for 2050. Write an essay describing the information and suggesting what the potential global impact could be if the 2050 projections are correct. Write 200 words.

The diagram below shows the global population by age in 1950 and 2000, and projected population figures for 2050. Write an essay describing the information and suggesting what the potential global impact could be if the 2050 projections are correct.

Population by Age Group

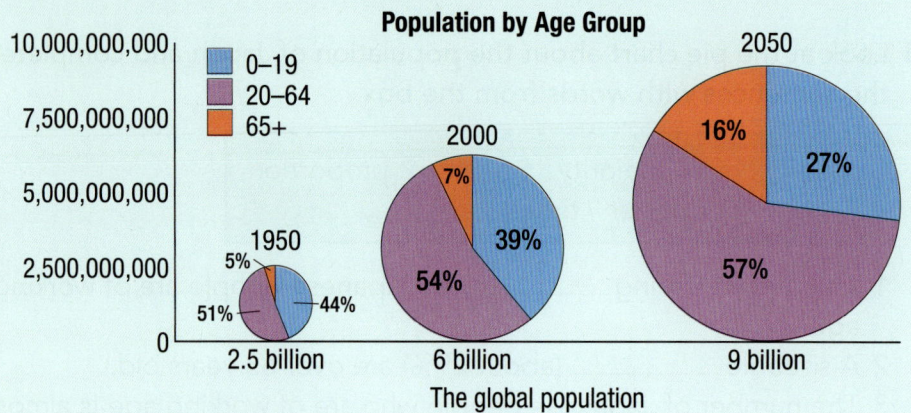

Legend:
- 0–19
- 20–64
- 65+

1950: 2.5 billion — 5%, 51%, 44%
2000: 6 billion — 7%, 39%, 54%
2050: 9 billion — 16%, 27%, 57%

Y-axis: 0, 2,500,000,000, 5,000,000,000, 7,500,000,000, 10,000,000,000

X-axis: The global population

2 Complete the plan for the essay below.

Introduce the diagram What is the chart about? What kind of diagram is it? What does the X and Y axis tell us?	
Describe the main trends How has the data changed over time? What does the smallest percentage show us? What does the largest percentage show us? What is the data to support this?	
What is the global impact of these predictions? What affect may this have on jobs, housing, care for the elderly etc.?	

3 Compare your answers with a partner. Did you focus on the same data?

WRITING TASK

Describe population trends in Japan. Use the data from the graph as evidence to support your claims. Suggest the potential impact on the country if the 2050 projections are correct. Write 350 to 400 words.

Japan: Population by age range in millions, 1950-2050 estimate (as of January 2022)

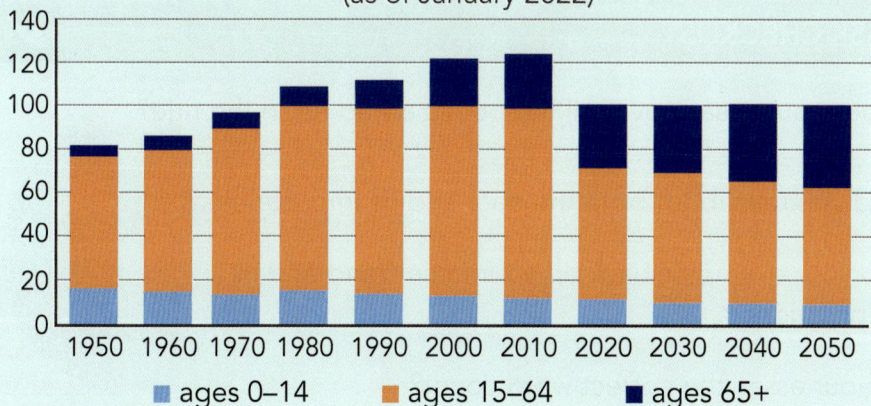

Source: *Japan Statistical Yearbook*

PLAN

1 Look again at the structure of the essay in Reading 2, which describes the impact of a young population on society in Saudi Arabia. You are going to write a similar essay about the impact of an ageing generation on Japan.

2 Discuss your ideas with a partner and make notes using the structure below. The word count for each paragraph is only a guide.

Introduction (50 words)
What is the topic of your essay? Write a thesis statement.
Description of the chart (100 words)
What are the main trends you want to discuss? What is the data to support this? (Look back at Exercise 2 on page 186.)
Projection for 2050 (100 words)
What would the negative impact on society be? Look back at your notes from the Critical thinking section.
Projection for 2050 (100 words)
What would the positive impact on society be? Look back at your notes from the Critical thinking section.
Conclusion (50 words)
Summarize your main ideas.

3 Use your notes and the task checklist below to write your first draft.

REVISE

4 Use the Task checklist to review your essay for content and structure.

TASK CHECKLIST	✔
Does your essay cover all the points asked for in the title?	
Did you talk about both the data and its implications?	
Do your examples back up your main trend and its implications?	
Is your essay the correct word count?	

5 Make any necessary changes to your essay.

EDIT

6 Use the Language checklist to edit your essay for language errors.

LANGUAGE CHECKLIST	✔
Did you include a sufficient range of appropriate topic-specific and academic language?	
Did you use a range of different numerical words and phrases to interpret the data? Are the phrases accurate?	
Did you use language of prediction including the first conditional, where appropriate?	
Did you use cause and effect phrases?	

7 Make any necessary changes to your essay.

OBJECTIVES REVIEW

1 Check your learning objectives for this unit. Write *3*, *2* or *1* for each objective.

3 = very well   2 = well   1 = not so well

I can ...

watch and understand a video about growing old.   _____

identify evidence in a text.   _____

draw appropriate conclusions from graphical data.   _____

use verb phrases to show cause and effect.   _____

use language of prediction.   _____

use the first conditional.   _____

use numerical words and phrases.   _____

interpret graphs and charts.   _____

write an analysis essay.   _____

2 Use the *Unlock* Digital Workbook for more practice with this unit's learning objectives.

UNLOCK
DIGITAL
WORKBOOK

WORDLIST

a range of (n phr) ⊙	focus on (phr v) ⊙	pension (n) ⊙
adapt (v) ⊙	in brief (n phr) ⊙	proportion (n) ⊙
capacity (n) ⊙	in contrast (n phr) ⊙	range (n) ⊙
cope (v) ⊙	in theory (n phr) ⊙	sum up (phr v) ⊙
demographic (adj)	leisure (n) ⊙	undertake (v) ⊙
documented (adj)	median (adj)	voluntary (adj)

⊙ = high-frequency words in the Cambridge Academic Corpus

GLOSSARY

⊙ = high-frequency words in the Cambridge Academic Corpus

Vocabulary	Pronunciation	Part of speech	Definition
UNIT 1			
confuse ⊙	/kən'fjuːz/	(v)	to mix up someone's mind or ideas, or to make something difficult to understand
consumption ⊙	/kən'sʌmpʃən/	(n)	the amount of something that someone uses, eats or drinks
continue ⊙	/kən'tɪnjuː/	(v)	to keep happening, existing or doing something, or to cause something or someone to do this
convenience ⊙	/kən'viːniəns/	(n)	the state of being suitable for your purposes and causing the least difficulty
discount ⊙	/'dɪskaʊnt/	(n)	a reduction in the usual price
domestic	/də'mestɪk/	(adj)	relating to a person's own country
dominant	/'dɒmɪnənt/	(adj)	more important, stronger or more noticeable than anything else of the same type
ensure ⊙	/ɪn'ʃɔː/	(v)	to make certain that something is done or happens
exclude ⊙	/ɪk'skluːd/	(v)	to prevent someone or something from entering a place or taking part in an activity
exhaust ⊙	/ɪg'zɔːst/	(v)	to use something completely
experiment ⊙	/ɪk'sperɪmənt/	(v)	to test or to try a new way of doing something
increase ⊙	/ɪn'kriːs/	(v)	to become larger or greater
inflation ⊙	/ɪn'fleɪʃən/	(n)	a continuing rise in prices in an economy
influence ⊙	/'ɪnfluəns/	(n)	the power to have an effect on people or things or someone or something which is able to do this
monopoly ⊙	/mə'nɒpəli/	(n)	complete control of something, especially an area of business, so that others have no share

Vocabulary	Pronunciation	Part of speech	Definition
multinational	/ˌmʌltiˈnæʃənəl/	(adj)	operating in different countries
outlet ⊙	/ˈaʊtlet/	(n)	a shop that is one of many owned by a particular company selling the goods produced by the company
refuse ⊙	/rɪˈfjuːz/	(v)	to say that you will not do or accept something
relatively	/ˈrelətɪvli/	(adv)	quite good, bad, etc. in comparison with other similar things or with what you expect
remove ⊙	/rɪˈmuːv/	(v)	to take something or someone away from somewhere, or off something
reputation ⊙	/ˌrepjəˈteɪʃən/	(n)	the general opinion that people have about someone or something based on their character in the past
selling point	/ˈselɪŋ pɔɪnt/	(n)	a feature that persuades people to buy a product
specialty ⊙	/ˈspeʃəlti/	(n)	a product that a place is especially known for
study ⊙	/ˈstʌdi/	(v)	to examine something very carefully
supplier ⊙	/səˈplaɪə/	(n)	a person or company that provides goods of a particular kind

UNIT 2

Vocabulary	Pronunciation	Part of speech	Definition
alternative ⊙	/ɒlˈtɜːnətɪv/	(n)	something that is different, especially from what is usual; a choice
aspect ⊙	/ˈæspekt/	(n)	a feature of something
assignment ⊙	/əˈsaɪnmənt/	(n)	a written essay at university
campus ⊙	/ˈkæm.pəs/	(n)	the buildings of a college or university and the land that surrounds them
community ⊙	/kəˈmjuːnəti/	(n)	the people living in the same area
concrete	/ˈkɒŋkriːt/	(adj)	based on actual things and particular examples
core	/kɔː/	(adj)	central, basic
core principles	/kɔː prɪnsəpəl/	(n phr)	key values
credible alternative	/ˈkredəbəl ɒlˈtɜːnətɪv /	(n phr)	a reliable substitute
deadline	/ˈded.laɪn/	(n)	a time or day by which something must be done

Vocabulary	Pronunciation	Part of speech	Definition
degree ⊙	/dɪˈɡriː/	(n)	a course of study at a college or university, or the qualification given to a student after he or she has completed his or her studies
discipline ⊙	/ˈdɪsəplɪn/	(n)	a particular area of study
dissertation ⊙	/ˌdɪsəˈteɪʃən/	(n)	a long essay usually for a university degree
distance learning	/ˈdɪstəns ˈlɜːnɪŋ/	(n phr)	general education from online teaching
employability	/ɪmˌplɔɪəˈbɪləti/	(n)	the skills and abilities that allow you to be employed
establishment ⊙	/ɪˈstæblɪʃmənt/	(n)	the act of starting or creating something that will last a long time
examination ⊙	/ɪɡˌzæmɪˈneɪʃən/	(n)	a formal test which students must pass to get a specific qualification
in-depth ⊙	/ɪn depθ/	(adj)	in a serious and detailed way
illiteracy	/ɪˈlɪt.ər.ə.si/	(n)	a lack of the ability to read and write
journal ⊙	/ˈdʒɜːnəl/	(n)	is a quarterly, peer-reviewed collection of research papers
lecturer ⊙	/ˈlektʃərə/	(n)	is the holder of a research position at a university who also teaches
modern phenomenon	/ˈmɒdən fəˈnɒmɪnən/	(n phr)	a recent trend
motivation ⊙	/ˌməʊtɪˈveɪʃən/	(n)	willingness to do something
online degree	/ˈɒnlaɪn dɪˈɡriː/	(n phr)	an academic qualification obtained from online instruction
peer ⊙	/pɪər/	(n)	a person who is the same age or has the same social position or the same abilities as other people in a group
plagiarism	/ˈpleɪdʒərɪzəm/	(n)	when students copy from or do not acknowledge their sources when writing an essay
principle	/prɪnsəpəl/	(adj)	a basic truth that explains or controls how something happens or works
pursue ⊙	/pəˈsjuː/	(v)	to try to do or achieve
regard ⊙	/rɪˈɡɑːd/	(v)	to consider or have an opinion about something or someone

Vocabulary	Pronunciation	Part of speech	Definition
semester	/sɪˈmestə/	(n)	one of the two periods a year is divided at college or university
seminar ⊙	/ˈsemɪnɑː/	(n)	an occasion when a teacher or expert and a group of people meet to study and discuss something
significant	/sɪgˈnɪfɪkənt/	(adj)	important, large or great
specific	/spəˈsɪfɪk/	(adj)	relating to one thing and not others; particular
stigma ⊙	/ˈstɪg.mə/	(n)	a strong feeling of disapproval that most people in a society have about something, especially when this is unfair
technological advances	/ˌteknəˈlɒdʒɪkəl ədˈvɑːnsɪz/	(n phr)	developments in technology
term ⊙	/tɜːm/	(n)	one of the three periods a year is divided at school, college or university
tutor ⊙	/ˈtʃuːtə/	(n)	the person who assumes responsibility for students' academic and personal welfare
virtual	/ˈvɜːtʃuəl/	(adj)	similar to real life but existing in a technological environment
virtual classroom	/ˈvɜːtʃuəl ˈklɑːsruːm/	(n phr)	online course

UNIT 3

Vocabulary	Pronunciation	Part of speech	Definition
adequate	/ˈædəkwət/	(adj)	enough or satisfactory for a particular purpose
adverse	/ædˈvɝːs/	(adj)	having a negative or harmful effect on something
burden ⊙	/ˈbɜːdən/	(n)	a duty or responsibility that is hard to bear
chief	/tʃiːf/	(adj)	most important or main
complex	/ˈkɒmpleks/	(adj)	difficult to understand or find an answer to because of having many different parts
consultation ⊙	/ˌkɒnsʌlˈteɪʃən/	(n)	a meeting to discuss something or to get advice
contribution ⊙	/ˌkɒntrɪˈbjuːʃən/	(n)	an amount of money that is given to help pay for something

Vocabulary	Pronunciation	Part of speech	Definition
controversial	/ˌkɒntrəˈvɜːʃəl/	(adj)	causing disagreement or discussion
conventional	/kənˈvenʃənəl/	(adj)	following the usual practices
diabetes ⊙	/ˌdaɪ.əˈbiː.tiːz/	(n)	a disease in which the body cannot control the level of sugar in the blood
drug ⊙	/drʌg/	(n)	any natural or artificially made chemical that is used as a medicine
epidemic ⊙	/ˌepɪˈdemɪk/	(n)	an illness that affects large numbers of people at the same time
fund ⊙	/fʌnd/	(v)	to provide money to pay for something
illegal	/ɪˈliːgəl/	(adj)	against the law
labour ⊙	/ˈleɪbər/	(n)	workers, especially people who do practical work with their hands
medical	/ˈmedɪkəl/	(adj)	related to the treatment of illness and injuries
mobility ⊙	/məʊˈbɪl.ə.ti/	(n)	the ability to move easily
obesity ⊙	/əʊˈbiː.sə.ti/	(n)	the fact of being extremely overweight, in a way that is dangerous for health
patent ⊙	/ˈpeɪtənt/	(n)	the official legal right to make or sell an invention for a particular number of years
pharmaceutical	/ˌfɑː.məˈsuː.tɪ.kəl/	(n)	a medicine
physical	/ˈfɪzɪkəl/	(adj)	connected with the body
physiotherapy	/ˌfɪz.i.əʊˈθer.ə.pi/	(n)	the treatment of problems of the muscles, joints, or nerves
precise	/prɪˈsaɪs/	(adj)	exact and accurate
prescription ⊙	/prɪˈskrɪp.ʃən/	(n)	a piece of paper on which a doctor writes the details of the medicine or drugs that someone needs
preventable illness	/prɪˈventəbəl ˈɪlnəs/	(n phr)	a disease that can be avoided, often by a person looking after themselves
professional	/ prəˈfeʃənəl/	(adj)	having the qualities that you connect with trained and skilled people
proponent ⊙	/prəˈpəʊnənt/	(n)	a person who supports a particular idea or plan of action
regardless	/rɪˈgɑːdləs/	(adv)	despite; not being affected by something

Vocabulary	Pronunciation	Part of speech	Definition
safety net	/'seɪfti net/	(n phr)	something used to protect a person against possible hardship or difficulty
substances	/'sʌbstənsɪz/	(n)	materials with particular physical characteristics
surgeon ◉	/'sɜː.dʒən/	(n)	a doctor who is specially trained to perform medical operations
surgery ◉	/'sɜːdʒəri/	(n)	the cutting open of the body to repair a damaged part
symptoms	/'sɪmptəmz/	(n)	reactions or feelings of illness that are caused by a disease
treatment ◉	/'triːtmənt/	(n)	the use of drugs, exercise, etc. to improve the condition of a sick or injured person, or to cure a disease
tumour ◉	/'tʃuː.mər/	(n)	a mass of diseased cells that might become a lump or cause illness
underfunding	/ˌʌndə'fʌndɪŋ/	(n)	the lack of money provided for something e.g. research
ward ◉	/wɔːd/	(n)	one of the parts or large rooms into which a hospital is divided, usually with beds for patients

UNIT 4

Vocabulary	Pronunciation	Part of speech	Definition
criticize ◉	/'krɪtɪsaɪz/	(v)	to express disapproval of someone or something
crucial	/'kruːʃəl/	(adj)	extremely important or necessary
devastating	/'devəsteɪtɪŋ/	(adj)	causing a lot of damage or destruction
disaster ◉	/dɪ'zɑːstə/	(n)	something that causes great harm or damage
emission ◉	/i'mɪʃ.ən/	(n)	the act of sending out gas, heat, etc.
extreme	/ɪk'striːm/	(adj)	very large in amount or degree
greenhouse gas ◉	/ˌgriːn.haʊs 'gæs/	(n)	a gas that causes the greenhouse effect, especially carbon dioxide
identify ◉	/aɪ'dentɪfaɪ/	(v)	to recognize something or somebody and say what or who that thing or person is
issue ◉	/'ɪʃuː/	(n)	a subject or problem that people are thinking about or discussing

Vocabulary	Pronunciation	Part of speech	Definition
large-scale 🔊	/ˌlɑːdʒˈskeɪl/	(adj)	involving a lot of people or happening in big numbers
long-term 🔊	/ˌlɒŋˈtɜːm/	(adj)	continuing a long time into the future
maintenance 🔊	/ˈmeɪntənəns/	(n)	the work needed to keep something in good condition
major	/ˈmeɪdʒə/	(adj)	more important, bigger or more serious than others of the same type
measure 🔊	/ˈmeʒə/	(n)	a method for dealing with a situation
policy 🔊	/ˈpɒləsi/	(n)	a set of ideas or a plan for action that a business, government, political party or group of people follow
reduction 🔊	/rɪˈdʌkʃən/	(n)	the act of making something smaller in size or amount
rely on 🔊	/rɪˈlaɪ ˌɒn/	(phr v)	to depend on or trust someone or something
severe	/sɪˈvɪə	(adj)	extremely bad
strategy 🔊	/ˈstrætədʒi/	(n)	a long-range plan for achieving a goal
sustainability 🔊	/səˌsteɪ.nəˈbɪl.ə.ti/	(n)	the quality of being able to continue over a period of time

UNIT 5

Vocabulary	Pronunciation	Part of speech	Definition
amenities	/əˈmiːnətis/	(n)	facilities that people enjoy living near, such as libraries, swimming pools and playgrounds
architectural	/ˌɑːkɪˈtektʃərəl/	(adj)	relating to architecture
architecturally	/ˌɑːkɪˈtektʃərəli/	(adv)	in an architectural way
architecture 🔊	/ˈɑːkɪtektʃə/	(n)	the art and practice of designing and making buildings
civilized	/ˈsɪvəlaɪzd/	(adj)	having a well-developed way of life and social systems
compromise 🔊	/ˈkɒmprəmaɪz/	(n)	an agreement reached between two sides who have different opinions, in which each side gives up something it had wanted
conservation 🔊	/ˌkɒnsəˈveɪʃən/	(n)	the protection of plants, animals and natural areas from the damaging effects of human activity
demonstrate 🔊	/ˈdemənstreɪt/	(v)	to show how to do something

Vocabulary	Pronunciation	Part of speech	Definition
depress ⊙	/dɪˈpres/	(v)	to cause someone to feel unhappy and without hope
depressing	/dɪˈpresɪŋ/	(adj)	making someone feel unhappy and without hope
depressingly	/dɪˈpresɪŋli/	(adv)	in a way that makes someone feel unhappy and without hope for the future
depression ⊙	/dɪˈpreʃən/	(n)	the state of feeling very unhappy and without hope for the future
durable	/ˈdʒʊərəbəl/	(adj)	able to last a long time without being damaged
efficiency ⊙	/ɪˈfɪʃənsi/	(n)	something that is done without wasting time, energy, or money
efficient	/ɪˈfɪʃənt/	(adj)	working or operating quickly and effectively in an organized way
environmental	/ɪnˌvaɪrənˈmentəl/	(adj)	relating to the environment
environmentally	/ɪnˌvaɪrənˈmentəli/	(adv)	relating to the environment
function ⊙	/ˈfʌŋkʃən/	(n)	a purpose, or the way something works
green belt	/griːn belt/	(n phr)	a strip of countryside round a city or town where building is not allowed
iconic	/aɪˈkɒn.ɪk/	(adj)	very famous or popular, especially being considered to represent particular opinions or a particular time
inspiring	/ɪnˈspaɪərɪŋ/	(adj)	giving you new ideas and making you feel you want to do something
outskirts	/ˈaʊtskɜːts/	(n)	the areas which form the edge of a town or city
reflect on ⊙	/rɪˈflekt ɒn/	(phr v)	to cause people to think of someone or something in a specified way
relevant	/ˈreləvənt/	(adj)	related to a subject or to something happening or being discussed
reputation ⊙	/ˌrepjəˈteɪʃən/	(n)	the general opinion that people have about someone
responsibility ⊙	/rɪˌspɒnsɪˈbɪləti/	(n)	something that it is your job or duty to deal with
responsible	/rɪˈspɒnsəbəl/	(adj)	to have control and authority over something or someone and the duty of taking care of it, him or her

Vocabulary	Pronunciation	Part of speech	Definition
second-hand	/ˈsek·ənd ˈhænd/	(adj)	not new; having been used in the past by someone else
sector ⊙	/ˈsektər/	(n)	a part of society that can be separated from other parts because of its own special character
skyscrapers	/ˈskaɪˌskreɪpərs/	(n)	very tall modern buildings in cities
structural engineer	/ˌstrʌktʃərəl endʒɪˈnɪər/	(n phr)	a person whose job it is to help build an architect's design
suburban	/səˈbɜːbən/	(adj)	relating to an area on the edge of a large town or city where people who work in the town or city often live
urban sprawl	/ˈɜr·bən ˈsprɔl/	(n phr)	the spread of a city into the area surrounding it, often without planning

UNIT 6

Vocabulary	Pronunciation	Part of speech	Definition
address ⊙	/əˈdres/	(v)	to give attention to or to deal with a matter or problem
aquatic	/əˈkwætɪk/	(adj)	living in or connected with water
consult ⊙	/kənˈsʌlt/	(v)	to get information or advice from a person, book, etc. with special knowledge on a particular subject
deliver ⊙	/dɪˈlɪvə/	(v)	to give
diminish ⊙	/dɪˈmɪnɪʃ/	(v)	to reduce or be reduced in size or importance
generate ⊙	/ˈdʒenəreɪt/	(v)	to cause to exist; produce
inexhaustible	/ˌɪnɪgˈzɔːstəbəl/	(adj)	in such large amounts that it cannot be used up
initial	/ɪˈnɪʃəl/	(adj)	at the beginning; first
instigate	/ˈɪnstɪgeɪt/	(v)	to cause an event or situation to happen
offshore	/ˌɒfˈʃɔː/	(adv)	away from or at a distance from the land
secure ⊙	/sɪˈkjʊə/	(v)	to get something, sometimes with difficulty
universal	/ˌjuːnɪˈvɜːsəl/	(adj)	existing everywhere or involving everyone
urgent	/ˈɜːdʒənt/	(adj)	needing immediate attention

Vocabulary	Pronunciation	Part of speech	Definition
utilize 🅾	/'juːtəlaɪz/	(v)	to make use of something
vital	/'vaɪtəl/	(adj)	necessary or extremely important for the success or continued existence of something

UNIT 7

Vocabulary	Pronunciation	Part of speech	Definition
abstract	/'æbstrækt/	(adj)	not of real things or people
acknowledge 🅾	/ək'nɒlɪdʒ/	(v)	to agree; to admit something is true
aesthetic 🅾	/es'θetɪk/	(adj)	relating to the enjoyment or study of beauty, or showing great beauty
avant-garde 🅾	/ˌævãː'gɑːd/	(adj)	relating to ideas and styles which are very original and modern
conceptual	/kən'septʃuəl/	(adj)	based on ideas or principles
contemporary	/kən'tempərəri/	(adj)	existing or happening now
deliberately	/dɪ'lɪbərətli/	(adv)	intentionally or in a planned way
distinction 🅾	/dɪ'stɪŋkʃən/	(n)	a difference between similar things
established	/ɪ'stæblɪʃt/	(adj)	generally accepted or familiar; having a long history
expressive	/ɪk'spresɪv/	(adj)	showing what somebody thinks or feels
figurative	/'fɪgərətɪv/	(adj)	showing people or things in a similar way to real life
lifelike	/'laɪflaɪk/	(adj)	looks very real
mechanical	/mə'kænɪkəl/	(adj)	related to machines
medium 🅾	/'miːdiəmz/	(n)	a material used to create art
moving	/'muːvɪŋ/	(adj)	causing strong feelings of sadness or sympathy
notion 🅾	/'nəʊʃən/	(n)	a belief or idea
objective	/əb'dʒektɪv/	(adj)	based on facts and reality
perceive 🅾	/pə'siːv/	(v)	to think of in a particular way
significance 🅾	/sɪg'nɪfɪkəns/	(n)	importance
sophisticated	/sə'fɪstɪkeɪtɪd/	(adj)	highly developed and complex

Vocabulary	Pronunciation	Part of speech	Definition
UNIT 8			
a range of 𝗢	/ə reɪndʒ əv/	(n phr)	a set of similar things
adapt 𝗢	ə'dæpt/	(v)	to adjust to different conditions or uses
capacity 𝗢	/kə'pæsəti/	(n)	a particular position or job; a role
cope 𝗢	/kəʊp/	(v)	to deal with problems successfully
demographic	/ˌdemə'græfɪk/	(adj)	relating to human populations and information such as their size, growth, ages and education
documented	/'dɒkjəməntɪd/	(adj)	recorded or written down
focus on 𝗢	/'fəʊkəs ɒn/	(phr v)	to give a lot of attention to one particular person, subject or thing
in brief 𝗢	/ɪn briːf/	(n phr)	lasting only a short time or containing few words
in contrast 𝗢	/ɪn 'kɒntrɑːst/	(n phr)	an obvious difference between two or more things
in theory 𝗢	/ɪn 'θɪəri/	(n phr)	if something is possible in theory, it should be possible, but often it does not happen in that way
leisure 𝗢	/'leʒə/	(n)	the time when you are not working or doing other duties
median	/'miːdiən/	(adj)	the middle number or amount in a series
pension 𝗢	/'penʃən/	(n)	a sum of money paid regularly to a person who has retired
proportion 𝗢	/prə'pɔːʃən/	(n)	a part or share of the whole
range 𝗢	/reɪndʒ/	(n)	amount or number between a lower and upper limit
sum up 𝗢	/sʌm ʌp/	(phr v)	to make a summary of the main points
undertake 𝗢	/ˌʌndə'teɪk/	(v)	to take responsibility for and begin doing something
voluntary	/'vɒləntəri/	(adj)	to do without being forced or paid to do it

VIDEO SCRIPTS

UNIT 1

▶ **China plans revival of Silk Road trade routes**

Narrator: We're up in the mountains near the border with Kazakhstan on China's far western frontier. The area we're travelling through is pretty remote, close to the furthest point from an ocean on the planet. This is the land of the old Silk Road where caravans of merchants trekked more than a thousand years ago at the height of China's imperial past. It's now at the heart of the country's plan to rebuild those ancient trading routes over land and by sea in one of the most expensive development projects ever attempted. This is a good place to come to understand the scale of those ambitions. Five years ago, there was almost nothing here. All of this has been built from scratch, including this brand new dry port intended as a key logistics hub for road and rail, alongside a vast new free trade zone. Mr Guo has big dreams for this project. He tells me Korgas could be the new Shenzhen or Shanghai.

Guo Jianbin: I think in three or four years, you will see the sky in Korgas will be more blue, and the city will become more beautiful and international trade will play a more key role.

Narrator: This is the 'build it and they will come' approach to infrastructure and trade: build the roads and rail links out into the region's developing countries and the trade will follow, so the theory goes. This huge cargo train is lumbering past us now on its way from China to Europe and this is very much the image of the modern Silk Road the Chinese government wants to project. But there's more going on here than just investment in infrastructure. This project is as much about politics as it is about economics. Ethan Cramer-Flood studies the project for an economic think tank and sees it as being driven primarily by China's domestic economic objectives and its broader geo-political goals.

Ethan Cramer-Flood: This is absolutely first and foremost err … a soft power initiative where it's clearly err … China has err … the leaders … leadership in Beijing and Beijing envisions the One Belt One Road project as being a significant, maybe the number one most significant part of Xi Jinping's err … so called 'China dream' and vision of … of um …

supporting the emergence of China onto the global stage as the next great superpower.

UNIT 2

▶ **Global literacy campaigns**

Narrator: At the 'School for Grannies', in India, the women can fulfil a lifelong ambition to learn to read and write.

Woman: I never went to school as a child, it feels great to come now, and study with my friends.

Narrator: The school may be unusual, but adult illiteracy isn't. The actor Idris Elba works with the global literacy campaign, Project Literacy, which aims to ensure that no child is born at risk of poor literacy.

Idris Elba: That ideology is about talking to adults. Most people think illiteracy is young people – it isn't. It's adults who live their life doing this. And now, they're too afraid to even say, or mention, 'Listen, I can't read.'

Narrator: Globally there are around 750 million adults who cannot read a simple sentence nor write their name. Fifty percent of these adults live in South Asia. However, the issue affects most regions. For example, 70 million adults in the United States have very low levels of literacy. Illiteracy often causes individuals to be disadvantaged and feel excluded from society.

Woman: When we used to go to the bank, we had to give thumb prints. It was embarrassing, and there was a stigma attached. Now I feel proud and happy because I can sign my name.

Narrator: Many adults who cannot read will try to hide their illiteracy from their family and friends.

Idris Elba: There's a lady called Wanda from New Jersey, and she couldn't read or write. She's got two young kids. And what she would do when the kids would ask her to sort of read a story-time, bedtime story, she would look at the pictures in a book and just make up the words. But she communicated to her children the love of reading books even though she couldn't do it.

Narrator: These are success stories, but statistically for children of parents who cannot read, the outlook is less positive. These children have below average literacy levels themselves and higher numbers drop out of school. Some turn to crime. Learning to read and write at any age is one way to end the cycle.

UNIT 3

▶ Doctors using VR to help patients

Narrator: Barcelona is a beautiful city to cycle through, and here at the Hospital del Mar, they remind their patients in the Intensive Care Unit of that each day. These doctors hope that virtual reality will make using physiotherapy bicycles in bed more bearable for patients.

Judith Marin: Our hypothesis is that using cycling will generate more benefits to our musculoskeletal system in terms of functional physiotherapy. However, adding the VR headset increases wellbeing and makes this physical therapy, which can be tough and complex for patients in intensive care units, more comfortable and pleasant.

Narrator: With 15 minutes a day cycling through the virtual streets of Barcelona, their patients may be able to restart their lives outside the ICU sooner. They're not the only medical team to recognize the value of escaping from reality.

Noel: It hurts a bit.

Narrator: 12-year-old Noel has a rare condition which means frequent surgery and physiotherapy to help him walk. Now researchers are using VR to help with that.

Ivan Phelan: Our biggest concern was how do we make walking fun.
So just keep walking down the road. Once you see those monsters, just try to aim at them.

Narrator: These days, Noel is killing monsters and escaping giant spiders while working on his mobility.

Noel: I don't realize how far I'm walking because I'm so concentrated on the game with my score.

Narrator: He now looks forward to his physiotherapy sessions.
A different use of VR experiences is helping patients understand the source of their pain. Matt Flanagan was one of the first chiropractors to use this method in the UK. He uses scans of his patients' spines to create a virtual tour for them.

Dr. Matthew Flanagan: There are lots of limitations with the old methods of communication and education. Umm, patients are not used to looking at anatomical models. And so often one of the things is patients find it difficult to know which is the front and which is the back …

Woman: It's almost surreal because you're in another world where you're looking at your posture, you're looking at yourself. It does motivate me to do the exercise because I can see the relevance of how it would help me get better.

Narrator: A similar VR application for cancer doctors has resulted from a collaboration between experts in the fields of cancer medicine, video gaming, and astronomy. They can use it to investigate an individual patient's tumour from the inside.

Dr Owen Harris: It's so much easier to notice differences, to notice features, to notice peculiarities when you're actually in a thing than when you're looking at it through a spreadsheet or a photograph. You see how a certain type of cell might be beside a blood vessel or a milk duct, and that might be important for the future prognosis of that patient.

Narrator: The team have shown that understanding the organization of cells in a tumour can help predict how a patient's condition might progress and respond to treatment.
Virtual reality headsets are becoming a more common sight in clinical settings. No doubt more creative applications of this technology are on the way.

UNIT 4

▶ Population and water

Narrator: We call our Earth 'the blue planet' because about 70% of the Earth's surface is covered in water. But most of that is in the oceans and seas. Just 2.5% is fresh water, and only 1% of that is available for human use. The rest is locked up in mountain passes and the Earth's polar ice caps. But there's another fact we need to understand about water.

Brian Richter: Well, there's no more water on the planet than there was when life first appeared on Earth. It changes its distribution, there's more water in different parts of the world than there were hundreds or thousands of years ago, but it's still exactly the same amount of water that's been here always.

Narrator: We use over half of all the available fresh water in the world to serve our needs: to transform deserts into fields, to produce energy from rivers and to build cities in some of the driest regions on the planet. But despite our creativity, there are many who have difficulty getting enough of this basic resource.

Brian Richter: More than a billion people on the planet already lack access to safe, clean drinking water. And we know things are going to get more difficult as the population continues to grow. Within the next 20 years, as much as half of the world's population will live in areas of water stress.

Narrator: Many water shortages are the result of poor infrastructure, politics, poverty or simply living in a dry part of the world. But more and more, they are due to increasing populations. Mexico City, for example, benefits from heavy annual rainfall. But its water system is stressed from supplying water to its 20 million inhabitants. The issue is the combination of leaks in the system and the fact that backup reservoirs are running dry. In Mexico City, shops that sell water for people's daily needs are becoming more and more common. But the water we use at home is only a small percentage of the total amount of water we consume. That's because of the huge amounts used by farms and factories.

Brian Richter: We may know where the water out of our tap comes from, but we very seldom know where the water that went into our can of cola or into the shirt that we're wearing on our back, where those goods were produced and how much water it required, and what the consequences were for the natural systems in those areas and for the local communities that are dependent upon that same water.

So for example, the cup of coffee that you may have in the morning requires on the order of 120 litres just to produce the coffee and bring it to your table. A hamburger, 8,000 litres of water, to produce enough water to grow the cotton in my shirt is 3,000 litres as well.

Narrator: The influence of humans on the world's freshwater systems is so significant that it can be seen from space. The Aral Sea, the freshwater lake in central Asia, once covered more than 25,000 square miles. But in the last 40 years, it has lost 90% of its water, with most of it going to support cotton farms. Lake Chad, on the southern side of the Sahara Desert, is now one tenth of its normal size due to drought and overuse. Yet, 30 million people still depend on it.

UNIT 5

▶ Government grants for warmer, cheaper housing

Commentator: Britain's got some of the chilliest buildings in Europe; £1 in every four we spend on heating is wasted due to things like poor insulation. Today the government announced it will extend grants for insulation work like this for warmer, cheaper housing for people who can least afford it.

Gareth Redmond-King: Emissions from homes have started to go up now, and that's a huge problem given the ... the scale of the challenge to reduce our emissions by 80% by 2050.

Um ... so at the current rate of err ... improving the energy efficiency of our homes we've calculated it will take us over a hundred years err ... to cut emissions from our homes.

Commentator: So, this is the sort of thing campaigners welcome, but worry whether the government will deliver on, with good reason. Cygnus Homes in Cambridgeshire build to the 'passive house' standard, engineered and insulated in such a way that just by living in the house it achieves a comfortable temperature, no extra heating required.

The energy bill for this house is about 75% less than the national average, and it can be built in less time by fewer workers than the traditional home. It shows that the construction industry can deliver the low carbon houses that Britain desperately needs, in very little time. So, why aren't we building them? Well because a couple of years ago in response to intense lobbying the government dropped something called the 'zero carbon home standard'.

As a result, housing developments with very efficient new homes like this one in Essex are the rarity rather than the norm. Even though innovative architects and developers say they can deliver them at a similar cost to more wasteful traditional homes.

So, the decision to scrap the zero carbon homes target, did that set everyone back do you think?

Tom Dollard: Undoubtedly yeah, it, um ... the industry had a clear target which was meant to be zero carbon homes at 2016 ... that was scrapped and ... and then there was a lot of confusion, there still is a lot of confusion, so ...

Reporter: So now there's an opportunity to put that back though, right?

Tom Dollard: Yeah, we need a clear target, um … simple policy to set house builders and developers a standard for zero carbon homes or low carbon homes whatever it needs … it just needs to be a standard.

Reporter: And you're saying in something like this shows that it can be done, it's within our grasp, it's not impossible.

Tom Dollard: Exactly.

Commentator: Today's strategy includes most of the things needed to deliver a truly greener economy. But, say critics, this government mustn't repeat the mistakes of others by giving up on green measures that long-term benefit consumers and the environment.

UNIT 6

▶ The power of the wind

Narrator: Wind power provides only about five percent of the world's energy needs today, but many environmental experts believe that figure could rise to almost 20% by 2030. Wind generates almost half a million megawatts of power – that's a 19% jump in just five years.

The UK is in a particularly good position to develop wind power because it is so, well, windy. At present, it ranks sixth in terms of capacity but is investing heavily in this renewable energy source. The percentage of electricity in the UK generated from wind power overtook that of coal, once Britain's primary source of energy, for the first time in 2016. The result was the lowest carbon emission rate since the 1920s.

The blades of the wind turbine turn a shaft, which passes the energy to a generator, which in turn transforms this energy into electricity. The wind is free, but the cost of power generation and storage actually makes wind power more expensive than traditional fossil fuel sources like coal, oil and gas. Smart technology is steadily bringing these costs down, however, and this trend is expected to continue.

There are two different types of wind power – onshore and offshore. Onshore wind farms are cheaper to build and maintain, but many people don't want windfarms in their areas. The turbines are quite noisy, and many people say they spoil the landscape.

Offshore windfarms, in contrast, are located in the sea, where few people care about their noise or appearance. The UK is a leader in offshore wind power. The London Array, off the east coast of England in the North Sea, is the largest offshore wind farm in the world.

The UK is also home to the world's first floating windfarm, off the northeast coast of Scotland. Although there is considerable public support for wind power, there is also opposition to these large, noisy devices. It's also important to remember that all of them are subject to changes in weather patterns. There are windy days and not-so-windy days. There are also not-so-windy years. Denmark, a leader in wind power, saw its wind power level drop in 2016 because of a lack of wind. Nevertheless, the shift to renewable energy sources like wind is likely to continue unabated.

Energy analyst: If you look at a more flexible, more dynamic energy system, with say more electric vehicles on … going out into the 2030s, then the backbone of that energy system should be cheap renewables. That is going to be the way to keep bills … bills low and you won't find an energy analyst out there that disagrees with that vision of the future.

UNIT 7

▶ Beijing Art Zone

Narrator: This was once a vast state-run military factory on the outskirts of Beijing, employing as many as 20,000 workers, complete with housing for the workers, athletic facilities, a hospital, and even its own orchestra. But that was the 1950s. Today, this factory complex presents a more peaceful and dramatically different face.

798 Art Zone became a space where artists could live and create art in a supportive community that included painters, sculptors, fashion designers, photographers and film directors. It attracted well-known Chinese artists, such as Sui Jiangou, whose dinosaurs are popular with visitors.

Visitors stop to examine and photograph these Red Metal Men, not quite sure if they are singing, shouting, staring in surprise or just hoping to catch some raindrops!

Although the Art Zone began as a place for outsiders, artists whose work was not seen in traditional museums, it has become a part of the mainstream arts scene, a popular attraction with both local visitors and international tourists. The centre hosts art exhibitions, annual film festivals, fashion shows, art auctions and theatre productions. And it has all the services common to other tourist destinations, including gift shops and cafés like this one, located in an old train station that used to transport materials to and from the original factory. It's free to the public and tens of thousands of visitors enjoy the centre every day.

When it began, the 798 Art Zone provided inexpensive living and workspace for struggling artists. Today the rents are high and only the most successful artists can afford to show their work here. The struggling artists have moved on to new locations – perhaps to the next 798.

UNIT 8

▶ **The happiest time of your life?**

Narrator: There's an old saying that your schooldays are the happiest days of your life. Wouldn't life be disappointing if that were true? Growing old is a common fear.

According to many researchers, it's a myth that youth is the most enjoyable, or even the healthiest time of your life.

Ageing comes with some significant benefits. A long-term study of 60,000 people in Australia, Britain and Germany found that we're at our happiest in our sixties and seventies – after we retire from work. One possible reason for this is that our relationships improve. We focus on the people we love and have more opportunities to be part of meaningful communities.

In our twenties and thirties, we may sacrifice the things that make us happy in order to climb the career ladder. However, as we age, we forget unachievable ambitions. Some psychologists believe this makes us less happy in middle age, but most agree that by our 50s and 60s we are better at accepting the lives we have.

Age also gives us new skills. Life experience teaches us to avoid things that make us unhappy. When arguments or problems arise, we have strategies to deal with them. Changes in our brains mean we are less anxious and less impulsive.

Our bodies and our brains improve, too. The immune system works best in our fifties and sixties, so we get fewer colds. Our bodies recognize viruses and deal with them more efficiently. Allergies too may disappear as our bodies adjust to our environments.

Although we forget more in later life, many mental abilities are better in our fifties than they were in our twenties.

Of course, there are disadvantages to ageing too. And in countries where there isn't a great deal of support for elderly people, poverty and loneliness may affect happiness. But if this research can teach us anything it's not to fear getting older. The best may be yet to come!

THANKS AND ACKNOWLEDGEMENTS

The authors and publishers acknowledge the following sources of copyright material and are grateful for the permissions granted. While every effort has been made, it has not always been possible to identify the sources of all the material used, or to trace all copyright holders. If any omissions are brought to our notice, we will be happy to include the appropriate acknowledgements on reprinting and in the next update to the digital edition, as applicable.

Key: U = Unit.

Photography
The following photographs are sourced from Getty Images.

U1: Oscar Wong/Moment; Marco Bottigelli/Moment; Kmatta/Moment; istetiana/Moment; Алексей Облов/Moment; mgstudyo/E+; filippo carini/500px; Georgijevic/E+; **U2:** vm/E+; Cultura RM Exclusive/Frank and Helena/Image Source; Monty Rakusen/DigitalVision; David Clapp/Stone; Kevin Dodge; Drazen_/E+; Natalia Gdovskaia/Moment; **U3:** Zorica Nastasic/E+; fcafotodigital/E+; Peter Dazeley/The Image Bank; SelectStock/Vetta; ljubaphoto/E+; **U4:** Bloomberg ; itasun/iStock/Getty Images Plus; JIJI PRESS/2011 AFP; JOE KLAMAR/AFP; Stocktrek Images; Andrew Holt/The Image Bank; Matt Cardy/Stringer; pop_jop/DigitalVision Vectors; Jill Schneider/Photodisc; **U5:** Salvator Barki/Moment; Wysiati/iStock/Getty Images Plus; Anna Gorin/Moment; Grant Faint/The Image Bank Unreleased; Buyenlarge/Archive Photos; George Rose/Getty Images News; Alexander Spatari/Moment; jhorrocks/E+; **U6:** Martin Ruegner/Stone; Justin Paget/DigitalVision; Lisa-Blue/E+; maginima/E+; praetorianphoto/E+; Arterra/Universal Images Group; pidjoe/E+; **U7:** Andrew Chin/Getty Images Entertainment; Dan Kitwood/Getty Images News; Chesnot/Getty Images Entertainment; Daniel Berehulak/Getty Images News; Jim Dyson/Getty Images News; © Marco Bottigelli/Moment; Peter Clarkson/Moment Open; ilbusca/DigitalVision Vectors; Victor VIRGILE/Gamma-Rapho; Jordan Lye/Moment; **U8:** Thanasis Zovoilis/The Image Bank; DAJ/amana images.

The following photographs are sourced from third party/other sources.

U7: © Association Marcel Duchamp/ADAGP, Paris and DACS, London 2024; Dan Kitwood; Jessica Hromas; © 2024 The Andy Warhol Foundation for the Visual Arts, Inc./Licensed by DACS, London.; © Damien Hirst and Science Ltd. All rights reserved, DACS 2024; Daniel Berehulak.

Front cover photography by CreativeNature_nl/iStock Getty Images Plus/Getty Images.

Illustration
U3: Oxford Designers & Illustrators.

Videos
The following video stills are sourced from Getty Images.

U1: Sky News/Film Image Partner; **U2:** AFPTV; WW News/Image Bank Film; kali9/Creatas Video; MartinHarvey/Creatas Video+/Getty Images Plus; mapodile/Creatas Video; **U3:** ITN; gorodenkoff; **U5:** ITN; **U6:** Sky News/Film Image Partner; Dorling Kindersley; Allstar Picture Library/Photolibrary Video; ITN; **U7:** piggyfoto/Getty Images Editorial Footage; ITN; **U8:** Caiafilm/Creatas Video; Thomas Barwick/Image Bank Film: Signature; Maskot/DigitalVision.

The following videos and stills are sourced from another source:
U4: BBC Worldwide Learning.

The following videos are sourced from Getty Images:

U2: AFPTV; David Sampedro; ITN; MartinHarvey/Creatas Video+/Getty Images Plus; simonkr/Vetta; Red Fish LLC/Image Bank Film; WW News/Image Bank Film; Yellow Dog Productions Inc./Image Bank Film: Signature; kali9/Creatas Video; Yellow Dog Productions Inc./Image Bank Film: Signature; Caiafilm/Vetta; Motortion/Creatas Video+/Getty Images Plus; **U3:** piola666/Vetta; Xinhua News Agency; Paul Barker/Getty Images Entertainment Video; ITN; PetroglyphFilms; nopparit/Creatas Video; Red Stock Studio/Creatas Video; gorodenkoff/Creatas Video+/Getty Images Plus; **U5:** AFPTV; Carl Court/Getty Images News Video; Pavel_Chag/Creatas Video+/Getty Images Plus; Thomas Knauer/DigitalVision; Nilang Kachare/Creatas Video; Andrii Bicher/Creatas Video+/Getty Images Plus; akinbostanci/Creatas Video; NurPhoto Footage; Carl Court/Staff/Getty Images News; Carl Court/Getty Images News; YOSHIKAZU TSUNO/AFP; **U8:** Lighthouse Films; ImagesBazaar/Photolibrary Video; MGM Library/Archive Films: Creative; simonkr/Vetta; Hiraman/Vetta; Jacob Wackerhausen/Creatas Video+; Klaus Vedfelt/one80: Signature; Wavebreakmedia/Creatas Video+; Caiafilm/Creatas Video; Prostock-Studio/Creatas Video+; pocketlight/Vetta; Thomas Barwick/Image Bank Film: Signature; Caiafilm/Creatas Video; Hiraman/Vetta; sturti/Creatas Video; Edwin Tan/Vetta; RubberBall Productions LLC/Photolibrary Video; shapecharge/Creatas Video; Andrii Iemelyanenko/Creatas Video+/Getty Images Plus; LPETTET/Creatas Video; Maskot/DigitalVision; Klaus Vedfelt/one80: Signature; AaronAmat/Creatas Video+/Getty Images Plus; FG Trade/Vetta; janiecbros/Vetta; recep-bg/Vetta; 10'000 Hours/Image Bank Film: Signature; andjic/Creatas Video; Mr. Big Film/Image Bank Film: Signature; Frick-ART/Creatas Video+/Getty Images Plus; SolStock/Vetta.

Audio
U8: Epidemic Sound via Getty Images.

Audio Production by John Marshall Media.

Typeset
Typesetting by emc design ltd.

Corpus
Development of this publication has made use of the Cambridge English Corpus (CEC). The CEC is a multi-billion-word computer database of contemporary spoken and written English. It includes British English, American English and other varieties of English. It also includes the Cambridge Learner Corpus, developed in collaboration with Cambridge English Language Assessment. Cambridge University Press has built up the CEC to provide evidence about language use that helps to produce better language teaching materials.

Cambridge Dictionaries
Cambridge dictionaries are the world's most widely used dictionaries for learners of English. The dictionaries are available in print and online at dictionary.cambridge.org. Copyright © Cambridge University Press, reproduced with permission.

UNLOCK ADVISORY PANEL

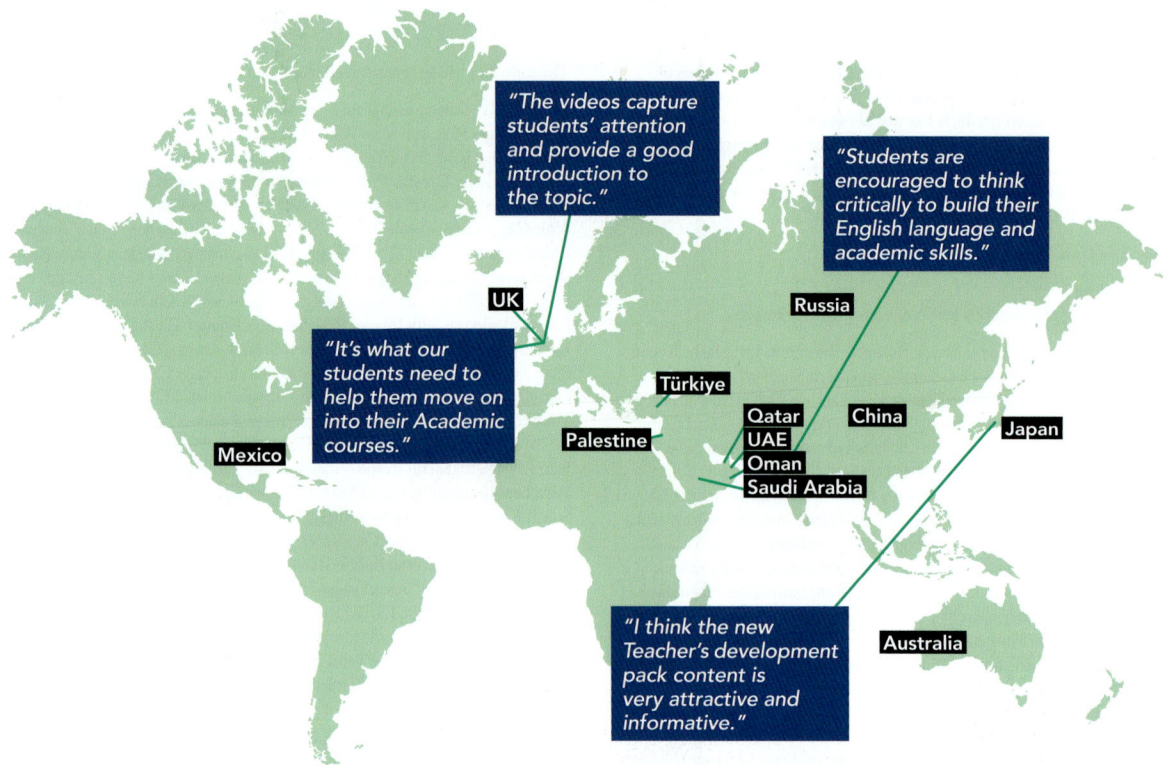

"The videos capture students' attention and provide a good introduction to the topic."

"Students are encouraged to think critically to build their English language and academic skills."

UK

Russia

"It's what our students need to help them move on into their Academic courses."

Türkiye

Mexico

Palestine

Qatar
UAE
Oman
Saudi Arabia

China

Japan

"I think the new Teacher's development pack content is very attractive and informative."

Australia

We would like to thank the following ELT professionals all around the world who contributed their expertise to *Unlock* Second Edition. Their insights then have continued to inform the development of *Unlock* Third Edition.

Adnan Abu Ayyash, Birzeit University, Palestine	Takayuki Hara, Kagoshima University, Japan	Megan Putney, Dhofar University, Oman
Bradley Adrain, University of Queensland, Australia	Esengül Hasdemir, Atilim University, Türkiye	Wayne Rimmer, United Kingdom
Sarah Ali, Nottingham Trent International College (NTIC), United Kingdom	Irina Idilova, Moscow Institute of Physics and Technology, Russia	Sana Salam, TED University, Türkiye
Ana Maria Astiazaran, Colegio Regis La Salle, Mexico	Meena Inguva, Sultan Qaboos University, Oman	Setenay Şekercioğlu, Işık University, Türkiye
Asmaa Awad, University of Sharjah, United Arab Emirates	Vasilios Konstantinidis, Prince Sultan University, Kingdom of Saudi Arabia	Robert B. Staehlin, Morioka University, Japan
Jesse Balanyk, Zayed University, United Arab Emirates	Andrew Leichsenring, Tamagawa University, Japan	Yizhi Tang, Xueersi English, TAL Group, China
Lenise Butler, Universidad del Valle de México, Mexico	Alexsandra Minic, Modern College of Business and Science, Oman	Valeria Thomson, Muscat College, Oman
Esin Çağlayan, Izmir University of Economics, Türkiye	Daniel Newbury, Fuji University, Japan	Amira Traish, University of Sharjah, United Arab Emirates
Matthew Carey, Qatar University, Qatar	Güliz Özgürel, Yaşar University, Türkiye	Poh Leng Wendelkin, INTO City, University of London, United Kingdom
Eileen Dickens, Universidad de las Américas, Mexico	Özlem Perks, Istanbul Ticaret University, Türkiye	Yoee Yang, The Affiliated High School of SCNU, China
Mireille Bassam Farah, United Arab Emirates	Claudia Piccoli, Harmon Hall, Mexico	Rola Youhia, University of Adelaide College, Australia
Adriana Ghoul, Arab American University, Palestine	Tom Pritchard, University of Edinburgh, United Kingdom	Long Zhao, Xueersi English, TAL Group, China
Burçin Gönülsen, Işık University, Türkiye		